Jennifer Lobo Meeks

Allegory in Early Greek Philosophy

STUDIES IN HISTORICAL PHILOSOPHY

Editor: Alexander Gungov
Consulting Editor: Donald Phillip Verene

ISSN 2629-0316

1   *Dustin Peone*
    Memory as Philosophy
    The Theory and Practice of Philosophical Recollection
    ISBN 978-3-8382-1336-1

2   *Raymond Barfield*
    The Poetic Apriori: Philosophical Imagination in a Meaningful Universe
    ISBN 978-3-8382-1350-7

3   *Jennifer Lobo Meeks*
    Allegory in Early Greek Philosophy
    ISBN 978-3-8382-1425-2

Jennifer Lobo Meeks

ALLEGORY IN
EARLY GREEK PHILOSOPHY

Bibliografische Information der Deutschen Nationalbibliothek

Die Deutsche Nationalbibliothek verzeichnet diese Publikation in der Deutschen Nationalbibliografie; detaillierte bibliografische Daten sind im Internet über http://dnb.d-nb.de abrufbar.

Bibliographic information published by the Deutsche Nationalbibliothek

Die Deutsche Nationalbibliothek lists this publication in the Deutsche Nationalbibliografie; detailed bibliographic data are available in the Internet at http://dnb.d-nb.de.

ISBN-13: 978-3-8382-1425-2
© *ibidem*-Verlag, Stuttgart 2020
Alle Rechte vorbehalten

Das Werk einschließlich aller seiner Teile ist urheberrechtlich geschützt. Jede Verwertung außerhalb der engen Grenzen des Urheberrechtsgesetzes ist ohne Zustimmung des Verlages unzulässig und strafbar. Dies gilt insbesondere für Vervielfältigungen, Übersetzungen, Mikroverfilmungen und elektronische Speicherformen sowie die Einspeicherung und Verarbeitung in elektronischen Systemen.

All rights reserved. No part of this publication may be reproduced, stored in or introduced into a retrieval system, or transmitted, in any form, or by any means (electronic, mechanical, photocopying, recording or otherwise) without the prior written permission of the publisher. Any person who does any unauthorized act in relation to this publication may be liable to criminal prosecution and civil claims for damages.

Printed in the EU

To Amara and Elena

Allegory is a manner of speech
denoting one thing by the letter of the words,
but another by their meaning.

Rhetorica ad Herennium
4.34.46

Contents

Preface 9

Chapter 1
Introduction: Speaking Wisdom Otherwise 11
    A Concise History of Allegory 11
    Myth, Philosophy, and the Speculative Task 22
    The Shift from *Muthos* to *Logos* 33

Chapter 2
The Presocratics and the Beginnings of Allegory 41
    Historical and Theoretical Considerations 41
    Philosophical Anticipations in Archaic Poetry 49
    The Three Senses of a Presocratic "Poetics" 58
    Presocratic Allegorical Practices 66

Chapter 3
Plato on Poetry, Myth, and Allegory 79
    Philosophical Myth in Plato's Dialogues 79
    The Ancient Quarrel with the Poets 86
    Imagination, Memory, and Resolution of the Quarrel 93
    "Other Speech" in Platonic Thought 100

Selected Bibliography 113

Index 121

Preface

Allegory says one thing, but means another. In philosophical discourse, which attempts to achieve clarity and precision of both language and thought, what purpose could such a technique possibly serve? We find allegory in its complementary procedures of interpretation and composition employed in almost every period in the history of philosophy. It appears simultaneously with the birth of philosophy in ancient Greece and remains dominant throughout most of classical antiquity. Toward the end of this period, it is adopted by Christian, Jewish, and Islamic thinkers and gradually becomes one of the most salient philosophical and literary tools of Medieval thought. Allegory continues to flourish during the Renaissance, in large part due to the classicist tendencies of the time, and it persists well into the early modern era. Only in the Romantic movement of the eighteenth and nineteenth centuries does allegory suffer a decline, as it comes to be seen as inferior in both its form and content to the symbol. Allegory has reemerged in contemporary thought in various literary criticism movements, with the result that its role and significance in philosophy has been not only reconceived but also revalued.

In this work, I consider the role that allegory plays in early Greek thought, particularly in the transition from the mythic tradition of the archaic poets to the philosophical traditions of the Presocratics and Plato. My purpose is to explore how a mode of speech that "says one thing, but means another" could be integral to philosophy, which otherwise seeks to achieve clarity and precision in its discourse. Allegory, in both its interpretative and compositional strains, allows philosophy to render myth self-conscious, thereby fulfilling the speculative task of narrating the whole of reality in a way that utilizes both reason and the imagination. In providing the earliest Greek thinkers, the Presocratics, with a way of both defending and appropriating the poetic wisdom of their predecessors, allegory enables philosophy to locate and recover its own origins in the mythic tradition.

Allegory allows philosophy simultaneously to move beyond *muthos* and express the whole in terms of *logos*, a rational account in which reality is represented in a more abstract and universal way than myth allows. With regard to Plato, my account of allegory seeks to reconcile his critique, formulated in the ancient quarrel between the poets and philosophers, with his frequent use of "other speech" in the dialogues. This reconciliation is accomplished by consideration of the role that imagination plays in his thought as well as the unique construction and function of his "philosophical myth."

This work is the result of many years of studying the history of philosophy, first at Loyola Marymount University, then at Université Paris-Sorbonne and later at Emory University, supported in some years by Fulbright and Mellon fellowships. It grew out of a longtime interest in the intersection of philosophy and poetry, and specifically in the poetic nature of early Greek philosophy. Writing even a short book is a solitary journey, but one made easier when surrounded by the support of family and friends. In addition to such support, I especially thank the classicist R. Bracht Branham and the philosopher Donald Phillip Verene for their advice on this project over a long period of time. I very much thank Molly Black Verene for her copyediting of the final version of the manuscript.

Without the encouragement of my parents, Christopher and Agnes Lobo, and my sister, Gillian Lobo, this work would have not been possible. I am ever grateful for the support of my husband, Anthony Meeks, who has surpassed all expectations that one might hope for in a spouse. Finally, I put forth this work to my two daughters, Amara and Elena, my unknowing muses in all things—past, present, and future.

Chapter 1
Introduction: Speaking Wisdom Otherwise

> Allegory, in some sense, belongs not to medieval man,
> but to man, or even to mind in general.
> It is of the very nature of thought and language
> to represent what is immaterial in picturable terms.
> C. S. Lewis, *The Allegory of Love*

A Concise History of Allegory

The etymology of the term allegory (*allegoria*) is a natural starting point for a discussion of its historical development. *Allegoria* has two component parts in ancient Greek. The first component, which comes from the adjective *allos*, means "other"; the second component, which comes from the verb *agourein*, originally meant "to speak in the assembly," or in the *agora*. Eventually the verb *agourein* is translated simply "to speak," but it is important to keep in mind its original connotation of public speech. In ancient Greek, the *agora* referred to both the official assembly and the open market. *Agourein* could thus denote either the official speech associated with the assembly or the common speech practiced in the marketplace. When combined with the prefix *allos*, both of these types of speech are inverted. The speech becomes "other" than what is said officially or commonly. It becomes secret or clandestine, on the one hand, and unworthy of or unsuitable for the crowd, on the other hand. In this way, allegory comes to suggest guarded or elite speech, depending on the context in which it is utilized. The sense of allegory as secret or guarded language was of particular use to the political allegorist, for whom it offered some freedom and protection from the exigencies of the official assembly. The religious or philosophical allegorist could also exploit the sense of allegory as elite or superior language in order to elevate his discourse above the common speech of the marketplace.

This etymological gloss of the term *allegoria* is significant because it also explains how its two traditions emerged over time. The tradition of allegorical composition stems from the practice of speaking otherwise (*allos* + *agourein*). Insofar as the emphasis here is placed on *saying* other than what is meant, the tradition of allegorical composition is in large part a rhetorical matter, focusing on the techniques involved in creating an allegorical text. This type of other speech implies and requires an audience, assigned with the task of interpreting its hidden or underlying meaning. Insofar as the emphasis here is placed on *meaning* other than what is said, the second tradition—allegorical interpretation—is largely an exegetical matter, focusing on uncovering the meaning from an already composed text. While both of these traditions become prominent in the literary culture of ancient Greece, they trace their roots back to the first philosophers, who employ allegory as a mode of interpretation of the poets as well as a compositional technique for their own original works.[1]

The practice of allegorical interpretation (*allegoresis*) emerged alongside the birth of philosophy during the Presocratic era. In the shift from myth to reason that characterizes this period, certain early Greek thinkers turned to allegory as a way to engage with their predecessors and with the poetic tradition as a whole. There is some debate as to whether these thinkers, as allegorists, were seeking primarily to defend the poets or to appropriate the poets' archaic wisdom for their own philosophical purposes. The classicist J. Tate argues for the latter: "Assuming that the myth-makers were concerned to edify and to instruct, the philosophers found in apparent immoralities and impieties a warning that both in offensive and in inoffensive passages one must look beneath the surface for the true significance of the tales."[2]

While Tate acknowledges the desire of early philosophers to defend the poetic tradition, he insists that philosophical allegory was originally positive, rather than negative, in its aim: "Those who wrote to defend the poets could, if they chose, make some use of the results of the allegorical method [of interpretation]; passages to which exception had been taken could be shown by allegorical treatment to be quite consistent with the view that the poets were wise and divinely inspired. But the first dim beginnings of allegory can be traced to another and weightier motive—namely, the desire of speculative thinkers to appropriate for their own use some at least of the mythical traditions."[3]

Arguing against this position, Kathryn Morgan asserts that the appropriation of the poets was of only secondary concern to these early Greek thinkers: "The first allegorists were defenders of Homer and the

---

[1] See Jon Whitman, "Appendix I: On the History of the Term 'Allegory'" in *Allegory: The Dynamics of an Ancient and Medieval Technique* (Cambridge, MA: Harvard University Press, 1999), 263-64.
[2] J. Tate, "Plato and Allegorical Interpretation," *The Classical Quarterly* 23, no. 3/4 (1929): 142.
[3] Ibid.

poets against philosophical attacks, rather than intellectuals trying to confirm their speculations through poetic authority."[4] Morgan concedes that the tendency to defend the poetic tradition gradually gives way to a less polemic attitude toward poetry and myth in general. This is particularly evident in the late fifth-century use of allegorical interpretation by the Sophists, who sought to make the authority of the great poets reflect their own philosophical endeavors.

During the Presocratic era, an incipient form of allegorical composition emerges with other early Greek thinkers. This is especially the case with Parmenides and Empedocles, who might be considered the first "philosopher-poets," given the poetic nature of their writings and their extensive use of allegory. Despite the emergence of both traditions at the dawn of Greek philosophy, the term *allegoria* does not come into use until much later, during the Roman period. Even though Plutarch is still referring to it as a new term at the end of the first century CE, the modes of discourse and thought to which the term is attached are already deeply embedded in classical thought by that point.

The allegorical impulse of the early Greek thinkers manifests itself as the search for esoteric truths and meaning in the works of Homer and Hesiod, who were thought to have possessed a wisdom that was concealed in their poetry, but that was ultimately interpretable. This impulse is also present in the work of the Derveni papyrus commentator of the fifth century BCE, who offers an allegorical reading of an Orphic poem and draws parallels between the mythic elements of the mystico-religious text and the philosophical views he wishes to advance. The seeds of Presocratic allegory can be further traced to Pherecydes of Syros and Theagenes of Rhegium in the sixth century BCE, who were thought to have made early attempts at allegorizing Homer in an attempt to discover philosophical insights hidden within his poetry.

In classical thought, allegory becomes synonymous with the concept of the symbol (*symbolon*), the oblique expression of a truth that is at once immediate and remote. Such a truth must be decoded for its under-meaning (*hyponoia*) so that its inherent enigma (*aenigma*) can be solved. This cluster of terms—*symbolon*, *hyponoia*, and *aenigma*—is closely associated with allegorical interpretation and composition during antiquity. Plato later finds this model of allegory problematic. He

---

[4] Kathryn A. Morgan, *Myth and Philosophy from the Presocratics to Plato* (Cambridge: Cambridge University Press, 2000), 98.

considers the poets as divinely inspired individuals. He concedes that they may attain to truth, thanks to the Muses, but it is truth grounded not by rational knowledge (*episteme*) but only by right opinion (*orthe doxa*). If this is the case, then an allegorical interpretation of their poetry is also necessarily subject to uncertainty.

The most that the interpreter can achieve is right opinion regarding the meaning of their work, and even this is subject to a certain degree of inspiration, particularly in the case of the rhapsodes. In other words, just as the poets follow no rational process in the composition of their works, but appeal to divine inspiration, so too does the allegorist work by inspiration rather than by reasoning from general principles. This renders allegorical interpretation inferior or deficient, in Plato's view. This position, however, is thrown into question by the fact that Plato himself regularly appeals to mythical narratives in his dialogues, which themselves seem to conceal philosophical truths and require at least some degree of allegorical interpretation.

Though not usually considered a pivotal figure in the history of allegory, Aristotle does contribute to its development as a philosophical technique, if only accidentally, in a number of his works. Aristotle had a conciliatory attitude toward the relationship between myth and philosophy, and this came to bear on both his views and practice of allegory. In contrast to Plato, Aristotle did not hold that philosophy implies a radical rupture with myth; rather, he believed that there was a certain continuity between what the archaic tradition imparted about the gods and what philosophy later had to say about them. For Aristotle, the philosopher is assigned the task of discerning the truths that were passed down in the mythical narratives about the gods—a difficult and often convoluted task—since these narratives contained only fragments of the original insights of earlier human civilizations. This task is accomplished through a sort of indirect or accidental form of *allegoresis*. Aristotle himself practiced allegory in various treatises, most notably in his discussion of the Prime Mover in the *Metaphysics*. But because his treatment of the philosophical import of allegory was linked to his rather obsolete view of tragedy in the *Poetics*, it was largely overlooked by thinkers in later antiquity, with the exception of certain Greek and Roman Stoics.

The Stoics were markedly influenced by Aristotle and were the only philosophical school of the Hellenistic period to develop an actual position on allegory. Between the early and the later Stoics, an important distinction is drawn between two types of allegory. The first includes material that is only accidentally or unintentionally allegorical; the second concerns material that is deliberate in its concealment of truths that are interpretable by the allegorist.[5] The first type appears to be constructed from Aristotle's views on allegory, while the second mirrors the model initiated by the Presocratics and critiqued by Plato. There is some evidence that the Stoics might have developed and even originated the model of allegory later adopted by the Neoplatonists. In this model, allegory is valued as compositional technique mainly because of its ability to conceal. By making obscure the wisdom expressed in a given text, allegory is a way of reserving that wisdom for a particular audience. The allegorist, then, is taken to be the initiate who moves from perception of the apparent meaning of a text to understanding its underlying reality. This initiate, for both the Stoic and the Neoplatonists, is the philosopher. The philosopher's task, unlike Plato's inspired allegorist, is to offer not a *translation* but a *commentary* of the allegorical text, which provides a way into the text without stripping it of its concealed wisdom.

The Neoplatonists reinforced the connection between allegory and the concealing and deciphering of esoteric truths. They also used both Homer *and* Plato as their primary sources, thus developing a hermeneutics directed at poetic *and* philosophical myths.[6] This is a significant moment in the development of allegory because it introduces the idea that even philosophical literature may be characterized by concealment and is ultimately subject to interpretation. Plato becomes for the Neoplatonists what Homer was for the Presocratics—a figure to defend and to appropriate. The Neoplatonists went one step further than the Presocratics in that they came to view Homer and Plato as more than just poet and philosopher. They were considered to be theologians, whose works were sacred texts, comparable to sacred writings of the Orphic and Chaldean traditions.[7] The Neoplatonic association of poetry and philosophy with theology also explains the motivations of the early Jewish and Christian

---

[5] Textual evidence for the first type of allegory is sparse, since only fragments remain of early Stoic works. The second type of allegory, on the other hand, can be traced back to the later Stoic, Cornutus, and his surviving work, *Theologiae Graecae Compendium*.

[6] Two examples of this would be Porphyry's commentary on the Cave of the Nymphs episode in Homer's *Odyssey* and Proclus's commentary on the Myth of Er in Plato's *Republic*.

[7] The best example of the tendency to theologize Plato is found in Proclus's *Platonic Theology*, an attempt to integrate ancient religious revelations (drawn from the Homeric and Hesiodic epics, the Orphic theogonies, and the Chaldean Oracles) into the philosophical traditions of Pythagoras and Plato.

allegorists during the Hellenistic period.⁸ These writers engaged in biblical exegesis as a way not only of syncretizing pagan philosophy with revealed religion, but also of reconciling inconsistencies within Scripture itself.

The preceding account gives some sense of allegory's development within the context of ancient Greek thought. However, allegory was also flourishing in the Latin West during this period as a method of both interpretation and composition.⁹ The concept of allegory first emerges with reference to the grammatical or rhetorical tradition, and it initially had the restricted sense of a trope, or a brief figure of speech. It takes on the sense of a sustained metaphor in both Cicero and Quintilian, and this is the sense it retains for the most part in later rhetorical traditions. From a historical perspective, the grammatical or rhetorical dimension of allegory is important. In the Latin substitution of the Greek term *hyponoia* with *allegoria*, there is a conceptual shift from meaning (*hyponoia* = under-meaning) to speaking (*allegoria* = other speech). While earlier Greek thinkers, particularly the Sophists, had recognized the value of allegory as a rhetorical ornamental device, the Latin reception of the term shifts the concept from the domain of philosophy to that of poetics. This shift complicates the development of allegory in later periods of the history of philosophy, beginning with the early Middle Ages in the Latin West.

The Medieval conception of allegory was strongly influenced by earlier Stoic and Neoplatonic treatments, but it also had to reconcile the notion of allegory as a simple verbal trope with the notion of it as something more profound, namely, the uncovering of esoteric or even sacred truths. This reconciliation was a direct result of the Latin rhetoricians' appropriation of the term and their emphasis on it as a compositional technique rather than an exegetical tool. As early as the fifth century CE, Medieval thinkers formulated a fourfold method of scriptural interpretation that sought to distinguish the loftier dimensions of allegory from its mere rhetorical function.¹⁰ The first element of this method is the

---

8   There are many thinkers included in this tradition, but two central figures are the Jewish philosopher Philo and the Christian philosopher Origen, both of Alexandria.

9   See Whitman, 264-66. Although earlier Greek rhetoricians, such as Demetrius and Philodemus, had purportedly used the term *allegoria*, the word's first Latin appearance is in Cicero's rhetorical treatise, *De Oratore*.

10 John Cassian, a Christian monk and theologian, provides the earliest formulation of this fourfold method in his *Conferences* at the end of the fifth century. More well-known, however, is Dante's presentation of the method in the *Convivio* and the *Epistle to Can Grande*, both written at the beginning of the fourteenth century.

literal sense, in which the events of a story are considered only for their historical significance, without ascribing any underlying meaning to them. The second is the allegorical or typological sense, which interprets this literal set of actions as being symbolic of certain other ideas or principles; in particular, Medieval biblical scholars engaged in this sense of allegory as a way of reconciling the Old and New Testaments. The third is the tropological sense, in which moral principles are drawn from the literal actions depicted in the story. The fourth is the anagogical sense, which interprets events in terms of their ultimate spiritual and prophetic significance.

This fourfold method of scriptural interpretation allowed Medieval scholars to elevate allegory above the realm of rhetoric while still preserving its unique literary function. It once again becomes the property of philosophy and, in the case of the Middle Ages, of theology as well.[11] Something akin to this also occurs in the tradition of allegorical composition during this period. Medieval vernacular authors explored both dimensions of allegory—as verbal trope and as theological truth—in order to compose works that lay claim to a greater authority than was usually afforded secular poetry. One of the primary techniques they employed in this pursuit was personification. Personification (*prosopopoeia*) was always an integral component of allegory, and its usage can be traced back to classical antiquity.

In the allegorical interpretation of archaic myths, deities and other figures were taken to represent certain cosmological forces or abstract principles. In the Medieval tradition of allegorical composition, personification inverts this interpretative process, in which the supernatural is rendered visible. It does this by expressing concretely, through the figures it employs, what is otherwise abstract or invisible, ranging from the virtues and vices to philosophy itself. In their emphasis on personification allegory, Medieval writers retain the rhetorical dimension of this genre while still using it to point to deeper philosophical and theological truths.[12]

---

[11] See J. C. Payen, "Genèse et finalités de la pensée allégorique au Moyen Age," *Revue de metaphysique et de morale* 78 (1973): 466-79. Payen writes: "Allegorical representation in the Middle Ages is much more than rhetorical ornamentation; it is a mode of apprehension of values that presumes a genuine revelation. Its aim is not limited to the systematization of doctrines; [rather], allegory is the veritable projection of thought into the spiritual realm" (467, translation mine).

[12] Personification was most notably employed in Prudentius's *Psychomachia,* but also in the works of later Medieval philosopher-poets, such as Boethius's *Consolation of Philosophy* and Bernadus Silvestris's *Cosmographia.*

Toward the end of the Middle Ages, all of these traditions coalesce: the ancient Greek allegorical impulse as the concealing and uncovering of esoteric truth, the Roman treatment of allegory as a rhetorical and stylistic device, and the Medieval emphasis on personification as a way of rendering abstract truths concrete. The humanism that comes to dominate Renaissance philosophy shapes its approach to allegory in a way that distinguishes it from earlier periods. In their rejection of scholastic monasticism, Renaissance thinkers began to stray from the exegetical method that their Medieval predecessors employed with regard to Scripture. Euhemerism, the interpretation of myths as actual accounts of historical persons and events, is also abandoned by some Renaissance philosophers, with the implication that sacred writings are interpreted as carrying little to no historical weight.[13] Others continued to attempt to syncretize pagan philosophy with Christianity. During this period, the practice of allegorical interpretation persists on the whole, but its scope as a form of spiritual empowerment diminishes.[14] With regard to allegorical compositions, the Renaissance is strongly influenced by the Roman treatment of allegory as a rhetorical device. This grows out of the revival of the Ciceronian concept of *humanitas*, which makes central the study of grammar, rhetoric, poetry, history, and moral philosophy.

The gradual abandonment of the Medieval exegetical method, and the return to the Roman emphasis on rhetoric during the Renaissance, signal the decline that allegory will suffer later during the Romantic period. It loses its transcendent power, its ability to point to spiritual truths hidden in sacred Scripture. As a trope, allegory is expected to achieve the ideals of clarity and directness, first introduced during the Enlightenment period, to be considered rhetorically valuable for Renaissance writers.[15] In the Neoclassicist literary movement that follows the Enlightenment, allegory is not quite rejected, but it is subject to more strict and formal

---

[13] See Rhodri Lewis, "Francis Bacon, Allegory and the Uses of Myth," *The Review of English Studies* 61, no. 250 (2010): 376-78.

[14] Marsilio Ficino's *Platonic Theology* is a good example of the type of allegorical interpretation that recalls late antiquity's attempt to syncretize Platonic thought with Christianity. Pico della Mirandola also sought to reconcile the metaphysical theories of his pagan and Christian predecessors in the *Heptaplus* and other works.

[15] See Mark L. Caldwell, "Allegory: The Renaissance Mode," *English Literary History* 44, no. 4 (1977) 580-600. Caldwell claims: "A more important feature of the [Renaissance] rhetorical tradition is its demand that allegory must be clear, the link between *litera* and hidden sense explicit. The trope must deliver its momentary force at once, then go its way without clouding the sense or obstructing the momentum of the argument of which it is, after all, only a part" (584).

parameters, such as clarity, symmetry, and fixed correspondence between the representation and its abstraction. While allegory persists into the Enlightenment, it is relegated to a position among other rhetorical ornaments, and its significance as a means of concealing esoteric truths in original compositions and uncovering them through interpretation is all but lost.

By the nineteenth century, the development of allegory is arrested through the emergence and ascendency of the symbol in both the English and German Romantic movements. The Romantic theory of the symbol grew in part out of the period's reaction against the Enlightenment conception of nature. Romantic thinkers viewed nature as a living, organic whole, imbued with beauty and mystery, rather than as a mechanical system governed by strict mathematical and physical laws. Engagement with nature involved "reading" it as a unified system of symbols through the use of the imaginative faculty. Another feature that characterized this period was a feeling of longing for the infinite, which nature itself seemed to express.

Romantics manifested this longing in their desire and attempt to express the infinite, or inexpressible, through their works of art and literature. This tendency can also be seen in their keen interest in the nature of myth. The Romantic study of mythology was not traditional in its approach; it did not consider myths as *allegorical* narratives pointing to certain universal truths or principles, i.e., as useful fictions. Rather, myths were *symbolic* narratives intimately connected to the experiences that give rise to them; they were conceived as expressions of absolute reality and, in that respect, they had the validity of absolute truth. This shift in approach was coupled with both the revival of classical mythology during the period and, for many Romantic thinkers, the elevation of mythology to a veritable science.[16]

These three aspects of Romanticism—its holistic view of nature, its longing for the infinite, and its conception of myth as symbolic narrative—give rise to the Romantic theory of the symbol. As previously mentioned, the term symbol (*symbolon*) had been associated with allegory since antiquity, and the two concepts were understood to be more or less

---

[16] This is evident in Friedrich Schelling's groundbreaking 1842 lectures on the philosophy of mythology. Of particular interest is his lecture on the allegorical interpretation of mythology. See F. W. J. Schelling, *Historical-critical Introduction to the Philosophy of Mythology*, trans. Mason Richey and Marcus Zisselsberger (Albany, NY: SUNY Press, 2007).

synonymous. During this period, however, allegory and the symbol become almost antithetical in both meaning and value. There is some debate as to how to regard the opposition between these two terms in Romanticism. Tzvetan Todorov maintains a strong dichotomy: "Nowhere does the meaning of 'symbol' appear so clearly as in the opposition between symbol and allegory—an opposition invented by the romantics and one that allows them to oppose themselves to all other viewpoints."[17] Against this view, Nicholas Halmi argues: "[The Romantic] opposition to allegory was, in fact, contrary to the impression fostered by the preoccupation of twentieth-century critics with the subject, neither widely nor consistently maintained" and, furthermore, "the formation of the Romantic concept of the symbol was *not* crucially dependent on a corresponding denigration of allegory."[18]

Goethe was the first Romantic thinker to contrast the two terms, and he consistently and categorically dismisses the allegorical technique for its instrumentality. He suggests that while the symbol can be considered an end in itself, allegory is the means, often artificial rather than natural, by which one can merely point to the end. Coleridge adopts and elaborates on Goethe's distinction between the allegorical and the symbolic modes. He defines allegory as the expression of a different subject, but with a resemblance, in that the symbol is the expression of the same subject, but with a difference. To express this self-establishing character of the symbol, both Coleridge and Schelling introduce the term "tautegorical," a concept that strongly influences later Romantic thinkers. For them, the symbol must be "always itself a part of that, of the whole of which it is representative."[19] Allegory, on the other hand, must be only suggestive of the whole, which, for the Romantics, ultimately relegated it to the status of a contrived sign that points to reality but does not embody it.

Allegory does not recover from its sharp decline during Romanticism until much later in the history of philosophy. Its revival is in large part due to the work of Walter Benjamin and Paul de Man during the twentieth century. Both sought to rescue allegory from the Romantic opposition in which the symbolic mode is preferred over the allegorical.

---

[17] Tzvetan Todorov, *Theories of the Symbol*, trans. Catherine Porter (Ithaca, NY Cornell University Press, 1982), 199.

[18] Nicholas Halmi, *The Genealogy of the Romantic Symbol* (Oxford: Oxford University Press, 2007), 12-13.

[19] Samuel Taylor Coleridge, *Miscellaneous Criticism*, ed. Thomas Middleton Raysor (Cambridge, MA: Harvard University Press, 1936), 99.

In his reinterpretation of the allegory, Benjamin appealed to the aesthetics of the German Baroque period mourning plays (*Trauerspiele*). This species of tragic drama, Benjamin argued, calls into question the possibility of meaningful representation in general.

The surrealistic signs employed in these mourning plays are "dead" in the sense that they offer no link between the particulars and their abstractions; in fact, their presence negates any such links. This negation signifies allegory's alienation from meaning rather than its access to it. There is a second movement, however, within allegory, which rehabilitates the sign. After meaning is destroyed or fragmented, it is then restored to a higher, allegorical level. This dialectical process is at the heart of allegory's authenticity. In Benjamin's view, the history of allegory through the Renaissance had concealed that there is a fundamental rift between the immanence of human life and the transcendence of abstract truth, but the Baroque *Trauerspiel* exposes this very chasm through its honest employment of allegory.

Rather than transferring to allegory the value that Romanticism had assigned to the symbol, Benjamin shows how that earlier concept was delusive and misconstrued. For Romantic thinkers, the symbol was intimately connected with their glorified notion of experience. Indeed, the symbol became for them the very expression of experience; it was perceived as perfectly self-sufficient and adequate in itself. Benjamin deconstructs this concept by arguing that symbolic representation is supposed to render present the absolute form in which a particular object participates. In doing this, the symbol would not only be part of the absolute form but also provide the perceiver with an intuitive and direct knowledge of this form. Benjamin argues that in the realm of the intellect, the symbolic link between the immanence of the particular and the transcendence of the form is impossible to substantiate, given the unbridgeable gap that exists between the realm of the ideas and the world of phenomena. This gap is exactly what the allegorical mode acknowledges and exposes.

By disclosing the fact that such a gap exists and that it is a fundamental part of the human condition, allegory becomes, rather than the symbol, a more authentic expression of experience. As Bainard Cowan points out, allegory is more than the outward expression of a sign that captures the experience of this ontological gap. It is also the intuition or the inner experience of this reality.[20] It is in this sense, during the modern period, that allegory comes to be reinterpreted and revived as not merely a rhetorical technique but as a philosophical mode of expression, with far-reaching epistemological and ontological implications.

Myth, Philosophy, and the Speculative Task

The development of allegory from the classical to the modern era reveals how inextricably it is bound up with its history, a topic more complex than any other in poetics. Unlike other tropes such as metaphor, metonymy, and personification, allegory signifies what lies behind and beyond the language it employs. This characteristic gives allegory a uniquely philosophical dimension—present in both of its modes—as a method of interpretation and as a means of composition. The role that allegory plays during the various periods in the history of philosophy is not random or arbitrary. Its prominence or decline during a given age points to the implicit and explicit ideological tendencies of that period.

The subject matter of allegory is vast and includes many different practices of writing, interpreting, and visually representing. Its use and evolution extends across philosophy, but also literature, art, religion, and culture in general. In these other areas, the history of allegory is complex and, in many instances, it mirrors the philosophical development of the technique. The allegorical meaning behind a literary work, for instance, can range from simple, as in the moral lessons captured in Aesop's fables or the parables of the Bible, to complex, as in the religious and political undertones of such works as Langland's *Piers Plowman* or Spenser's *The Faerie Queene*. In art and literature, as in philosophy, allegory is employed both to create works of a certain kind and to serve as a hermeneutic tool for understanding such works.

As an interpretative technique, allegory unveils the hidden meanings in various artistic (drawing, painting, sculpture, etc.) and literary (fiction, poetry, drama, etc.) forms. This technique is akin to the philosophical use of allegory to access the esoteric or sacred truths concealed in the figurative language of myth and Scripture. As a method of composition,

---

[20] See Bainard Cowan, "Walter Benjamin's Theory of Allegory," *New German Critique*, no. 22 (1981): 109-122. Cowan writes: "Transforming things into signs is both what allegory does—its technique—and what it is about—its content. Nor is this transformation exclusively an intellectual one: the signs perceived strike notes at the depth of one's being, regardless of whether they point to heaven, to an irretrievable past, or to the grave" (110).

allegory is employed by artists and writers alike to make the perceptual and conceptual shift from figure to meaning, from the particular to the abstract. Allegory is subject to the same rises and falls in the history of art and literature that it experiences in philosophy. As mentioned above, the prevalence of the trope during the Medieval and Renaissance periods is followed by its devaluation in Romantic artistic and literary circles, which turned to the symbol as the seemingly superior and thus preferred mode of expression.

The study of allegory as an aesthetic or literary technique, however, cannot adequately explain how it functions as a philosophical technique. The purpose of a given work of art or literature may be to report, to instruct, or simply to please its audience. Philosophy is a literary art in its own right, and all of the various forms of philosophical discourse may be said to constitute a unique body of literature with its own set of ends. What most distinguishes the philosophical from non-philosophical works of art or literature is that any didactic, stylistic, or other intention is inevitably and ultimately subsumed by a higher and more comprehensive end—to capture and express what is absolute in concrete and particular terms. To express the absolute sense of things is the goal of speculative philosophy.

Speculative philosophy (*philosophia contemplativa*) identifies the True with the whole and attempts both to grasp the True in thought and to narrate the True in language. The dictum, "the True is the whole," comes from Hegel, the preeminent speculative philosopher of modern philosophy.[21] Human beings have always been possessed of the speculative impulse, and speculation has been a part of philosophical inquiry and discourse, beginning with the first philosophers in ancient Greece. As Donald Phillip Verene describes it, philosophy pursued as speculation does not exclude other types of philosophical inquiry, such as critical reflection or analysis, but it differs from these approaches. Verene writes: "Critical reflection and analysis keep very tightly to those aspects of experience that can be understood, that can be ordered and classified. To speak about the whole the philosopher must stand common sense on its head and attempt what is in principle impossible—to glimpse the whole of experience from within experience, to have the divine perspective."[22] This attempt to glimpse the whole and to narrate it is first found in the myths that are at

---

[21] G.W.F. Hegel, *Phenomenology of Spirit*, trans. A.V. Miller (Oxford: Oxford University Press, 1977), 11.

[22] Donald Phillip Verene, *Speculative Philosophy* (Lanham, MD: Lexington Books, 2009), x.

the basis of every culture. The task of philosophy is to supersede the mythical. This speculative impulse gives rise to allegory, which is employed by the first philosophers as a way of narrating the whole in a self-conscious way.

The term speculation (*speculatio*) is derived from the Latin verb *specere*, which means "to look at, to view." In its philosophical usage, speculation is elevated to an intuitive, visionary, mode of apprehension. The meaning of the term suggests not only vision as such, but an intelligent and comprehending vision.[23] This intuitive yet intelligible grasp of the whole is associated with a feeling of wonder (*thauma*), out of which philosophy is traditionally said to emerge. One of the earliest accounts in which the connection is made between speculation as vision and philosophy is Plato's description of God's creation of human sight in the *Timaeus*. As part of his "likely story" about the formation of the universe and human beings, Timaeus explains that there are two causes that underlie the human capacity of sight.

The secondary or auxiliary causes deal with the physical dimension and mechanics of vision. The primary cause and higher purpose of sight is intimately connected with philosophical inquiry: "As my account has it, our sight has indeed proved to be a source of supreme benefit to us, in that none of our present statements about the universe could ever have been made if we had never seen any stars, sun or heaven. . . . These pursuits have given us philosophy, a gift from the gods to the mortal race whose value neither has been nor ever will be surpassed" (47a-b).[24] The power of sight gives rise to the power of inquiring about the nature of the universe, which in turn begets the practice and, eventually, the discipline of philosophy.

While rational speculation may not be said to exist prior to the birth of philosophy, the speculative impulse is present in primitive man. Primitive and modern man alike partake in the experience of wonder that accompanies apprehension of the whole. The term "modern" here is not restricted to a certain era; it is used only to distinguish between human beings belonging to the so-called "primitive" world and those who, in breaking away from that world, immediately succeed them. Both primitive and modern man pass from awe to anxiety as their speculations bring into

---

[23] See Henri Frankfort et al., *Before Philosophy: The Intellectual Adventure of Ancient Man* (Baltimore: Penguin, 1949), 11.

[24] Unless otherwise indicated, all citations from Plato's dialogues are drawn from John E. Cooper, ed., *Plato: Complete Works* (Indianapolis, IN: Hackett, 1997).

focus certain perennial concerns: their privileged yet precarious place in nature; their ability to control, or at least influence, the factors that govern their destiny; and their mortality as concretized through the fact of death. What distinguishes primitive and modern societies is that the former are often characterized as being embedded in the natural world and as possessing an immediacy of experience with this world.[25]

As Henri Frankfort points out, the idea that speculation transcends this type of experience, and is thus inaccessible to primitive man, is misleading. He asserts: "If we use the word [speculation] in its original sense, then we may say that speculative thought attempts to *underpin* the chaos of experience so that it may reveal the features of a structure—order, coherence, and meaning."[26] In this sense, speculation may be said to inhere in rather than transcend the human experience of the natural world. This clarification provides some insight into how and to what extent speculation was just as much a part of archaic humanity as it is a part of modern humanity.

What distinguishes primitive man from modern man, then, is neither that he lacks the speculative impulse nor that he is immune to the feeling of wonder that speculation arouses. Primitive man also seeks to narrate in language the whole that he has apprehended in thought. The difference between archaic and modern humanity lies in both the specific *content* of their narratives and in the *form* that these narratives take. Primitive man turns to mythico-religious accounts, while modern man turns to philosophico-scientific reasoning. Frankfort identifies two main ways in which the former type of account differs from the latter. First, the primitive speculation that is expressed in myths is not restricted by a disciplined search for truth, whereas this is precisely what characterizes and drives subsequent philosophical inquiry. Second, in the mythical mindset, the realms of nature and man are not distinguished, whereas in the philosophical attitude, these two realms are not only separated but often opposed.

---

[25] See Paul Radin, *Primitive Man as Philosopher* (New York: D. Appleton & Company, 1927), 229-56. Radin suggests that the commonly accepted distinction between primitive and modern man is dubious. He proposes a division along the lines of two temperaments, the practical and the speculative, which characterize the man of action and the thinker, respectively. As both of these "types" can be found to also exist in primitive humanity, Radin argues that they serve as a better means of understanding primitive man's approach to reality.

[26] Frankfort et al., 11.

This second point, according to Frankfort, is demonstrated by the fact that primitive man regards nature, or the phenomenal world, as a "Thou." This stands in sharp contrast to modern man's attitude towards this world as an "It." This fundamental difference is evidenced in the myths that serve as primitive man's way of narrating the whole. There are two main types of myth that provide superstructures of meaning and value for primitive man. The first type is the cosmogonic or cosmological myth, a story describing the origin of the world and everything in it. The second type is the anthropological or hero myth, which is a story describing the right way to live. Although the existence of these two different kinds of myth seems to indicate that there is a difference in primitive man's speculations about nature versus those about himself, Frankfort argues that this was not the case. On the contrary, for archaic humanity, nature and man did not stand in opposition to each other and did not, therefore, have to be apprehended by different modes of cognition. As a result, primitive man regularly conceived of natural phenomena in terms of human experience, and vice versa. An example of this may be found in Hesiod's *Theogony*, in which the stories of the world's creation, the origins of the gods, and man's relation to these gods and to other men coalesce to form a single, unified account of the whole.[27]

The primitive understanding of nature as a Thou puts man in an "I-Thou" relationship with the phenomenal world. Several features characterize this relationship and distinguish it from the "I-It" relationship that binds modern man and nature together. First, the familiar subject-object dichotomy that both underlies and drives scientific thought is nowhere to be found in mythic mindset. Man's experiences with the natural world unfold in these myths as stories of "life confronting life." Second, nature is not inanimate for primitive man; nature is a live presence with whom he enters into a dynamic and reciprocal relationship.

As Frankfort observes, nature as a Thou does not offer itself up as a passive receptacle for man's understanding; on the contrary, it *reveals* itself to man.[28] The third feature of the "I-Thou" relationship, then, is the

---

[27] See Frankfort et al., 12-36.

[28] On this point, see also Bruno Snell, *The Discovery of Mind: The Greek Origins of European Thought*, trans. T. G. Rosenmeyer (Cambridge, MA: Harvard University Press, 1953). Snell writes: "The truth of logical thought is something that requires to be sought, to be investigated, pondered. The mythical images, on the other hand, *reveal* to us of themselves their full content and significance. Mythical thought requires *receptivity*; logic cannot exist without activity" (224, italics mine).

personal nature of these revelations. They disclose nature in all of its individuality and its uniqueness. These revelations also explain why the particular-universal distinction carries little weight for primitive man, which is in contrast to the importance it holds for modern man. Since primitive man's speculations are subject to nature revealing itself to him, they do not aim at uncovering any universal laws or patterns that would transform the Thou into a static and lifeless entity.

The idea that primitive man's relationship with nature is governed by revelation is expressed in his narration of the whole. In ancient Greek myths this revelation is often mediated through the figure of the Muses. The poet or mythmaker begins his tale by appealing to the Muses, despite their ability to sing true as well as false songs. This appeal to an external authority underscores the first point that Frankfort makes in distinguishing mythico-religious accounts from philosophico-scientific ones. The former do not embody a disciplined search for truth. Mythic consciousness does not pursue truth as something separate from the practical quest to survive, the aesthetic pursuit of beauty, or the dramatic interest in mystery. There is a lack of autonomy that characterizes primitive thought.[29]

While primitive man may be capable of more than mere fantasy-thinking, his narrations are inevitably steeped in the imagination. In myth, imagery is inseparable from thought. The aim of myth is not to explain natural occurrences with the detachment or intelligibility that guides scientific accounts. This aim does not mean, however, that myth is an invalid or inauthentic narration of the whole. Frankfort concludes that myth is to be taken seriously because "it reveals a significant, if unverifiable, truth—we might say a metaphysical truth."[30] The metaphysical truth that myth expresses is none other than the speculative truth implicitly and intuitively recognized by primitive man, namely, the identification of the True and the whole.

Despite its lack of autonomy of thought, there is a certain logic that underlies myth-making (*mythopoeia*). Ernst Cassirer claims that mythical thought is a symbolic form and as such, it possesses "a particular way of

---

[29] See Radin, 275-91. Radin contests the claim that primitive thought wholly lacked autonomy and argues that primitive man engaged in speculation for its own sake. He concedes that this practice was limited to a small group of individuals, but argues that it nonetheless illustrates the beginnings of religious-philosophical systematization.

[30] Frankfort et al.,16.

seeing, and carries within itself its particular and proper source of light."[31] He distinguishes the mythical from scientific approaches to reality: "When we compare the empirical-scientific and the mythical world views, it becomes evident that the contrast between them does not reside in their use of entirely different categories in contemplating and interpreting reality. It is not the quality of these categories but their *modality* which distinguishes myth from empirical-scientific knowledge."[32] The question of origins (*arche*) is a central concern in mythopoeic thought, just as it is in philosophical thought. The empirical-scientific categories of causality, change, space, and time are taken up and expressed through myths.

In keeping with its view of nature as a Thou, the mythic mind deals with questions of causality by asking for the *who* rather than the *how* that underlies a phenomenal occurrence. Change is conceived as metamorphosis and does not necessarily require an intelligible process linking the initial and final states. Space is regarded as a coordinated system, just as in scientific thought, but in the mythic mind this system is determined by the emotional recognition of values rather than by an objective set of measurements. Time is understood in terms of experienced time, and the repetition of an event coalesces with the original event, thus explaining the importance of ritual in mythic societies.[33]

The most distinctive feature of the logic of mythopoeic thought is its multifaceted approach to reality. Verene describes myth as humanity's "first thoughts" and philosophy or metaphysics as its "second thoughts."[34] As the first complete speech, myth accomplishes the identification of the True with the whole, but it does so by incorporating the opposites inherent in reality into its account, rather than trying to unify them under a single rational principle. Myth also embraces a multiplicity of causes: "The categorical drive [of philosophy] toward the reduction of a multiplicity of phenomena to a single cause is for myth a poverty of thought."[35] These

---

[31] Ernst Cassirer, *Language and Myth*, trans. Susanne K. Langer (New York: Dover, 1946), 11.

[32] Ernst Cassirer, *Mythical Thought*, vol. 2 of *The Philosophy of Symbolic Forms*, trans. Ralph Manheim (New Haven, CT: Yale University Press, 1955), 60.

[33] See Frankfort et al., 19-36. On the category of time, see also Mircea Eliade's *The Myth of the Eternal Return: Cosmos and History*, trans. Willard R. Trask (Princeton, NJ: Princeton University Press, 2005).

[34] On myth as first thoughts, see also Barbara C. Sproul, *Primal Myths: Creating the World* (San Francisco: Harper and Row, 1979).

[35] Donald Phillip Verene, *Philosophy and the Return to Self-Knowledge* (New Haven, CT: Yale University Press, 1997), 219.

tendencies stand in sharp contrast to the philosophico-scientific approach to reality, in which oppositions are viewed as obstacles to overcome and multiplicity is to be avoided in favor of unity.

The wisdom of myth lies in its ability to recognize the unity that underlies the many guises in which phenomena present themselves. The metaphysical truth that myth expresses, according to Frankfort, "has not the universality and the lucidity of theoretical statement. It is concrete, though it claims to be unassailable in its validity. It claims recognition by the faithful; it does not pretend to justification before the critical."[36] This truth is speculative in its scope, but as it is embedded in nature and in the I-Thou relationship of primitive man with phenomenal reality, it is conveyed by means of the imagination rather than the intellect.

If these features of mythopoeic thought entail the dominance of the imagination to carry out and satisfy primitive man's speculative impulse, how does modern man satisfy this same impulse, once the mythic mindset is superseded by philosophical consciousness? His experience of the natural world is now guided primarily by reason, rather than the imagination. Nature becomes an object of detached scientific investigation; it is viewed as inanimate and impersonal, subject to predictable laws. For modern man, nature is no longer a Thou, a living presence who reveals itself to man through the immediacy of his experience. The mythical or supernatural element is for the most part replaced by natural causes. Reality is seen, from the perspective of modern man, in terms of a series of oppositions that must be reconciled. He seeks to do this by formulating a particular type of account—a philosophico-scientific narration of the whole.

Caution must be exercised in characterizing modern man, and particularly his relationship to nature, in such sweeping terms. The immediate successors of primitive man may indeed be called modern, but they are so in only a limited sense. The Presocratic thinkers of the sixth and fifth centuries, for instance, are certainly modern in contrast to their poetic predecessors, but they possess a very different approach to nature than their early modern counterparts of the sixteenth or seventeenth centuries. Similarly, both the totemic societies that predate classical antiquity and the ancient Greek poets, Homer and Hesiod, may be considered primitive, though there are obvious and significant differences between the ways in which each manifests the mythic mindset. It is

---

[36] Frankfort et al.,16.

reasonable to assert that the way modern man engages with nature represents a noticeable shift away from the immediacy of primitive man's experience. His approach becomes guided by reason and he sheds many of the restrictions imposed by a mythopoeic worldview. This fact neither diminishes the role that the imagination plays for modern man nor does it preclude him from being influenced by the mythic attitude in his conception of nature.

F. M. Cornford, in his study of the origins of Western speculation, takes the concept of nature to be at the very heart of the influence that primitive man has on modern man. He rejects the presupposition that the first objects of modern man's speculative impulse are the inner and outer experience of the individual standing in the presence of nature. To begin with such a presupposition is to assume that the first philosophers were occupied with the fields of natural science and psychology in a quasi-modern sense; this is both anachronistic and misleading. Cornford traces the origins of ancient Greek speculation back to certain notions that pervaded the mythical mind and that ultimately become entrenched in modern man's understanding of nature (*physis*). These are the religious notions of god, soul, destiny, and law. As Cornford asserts, "unless we have some grasp of that history we are not likely to understand the [origins of western] speculation, which, however scientific its spirit may be, constantly operates with these religious ideas, and is to a large extent confined in its movement within the limits already traced by them."[37]

From the first utterances attributed to the founder of Western philosophy, Thales of Miletus, there is already the intimation of a strong connection between modern man's conception of nature and the religious notions of his predecessors. Two main principles are attributed to Thales: the ultimate nature of all things is water and the world is full of spirits or gods. Neither of these propositions stems from Thales' "inner or outer experience" of natural phenomena. On the contrary, they are inherited from the mythic or religious worldview, in which nature was conceived as *dynamic*, as the primordial force or active energy underlying all things. This dynamism was coupled with another sense of nature as *static*, as the system of all phenomena in time and space and also as the inner constitution or essence of a thing.

---

[37] F. M. Cornford, *From Religion to Philosophy: A Study in the Origins of Western Speculation* (Mineola, NY: Dover Publications, 2004), 4-5.

The primitive understanding of nature's static aspect expressed itself primarily through the religious notion of destiny (*moira*). Anaximander, the pupil of Thales, is one of the earliest examples of how this primitive, religious notion is appropriated by the philosophers. It is noteworthy that his sole surviving fragment utilizes and relies on the concept of *moira*: "The source from which existing things derive their existence is also that to which they return at their destruction, according to necessity; for they give justice and make reparation to one another for their injustice, according to the arrangement of Time" (fr. 1).[38] Although the context of Anaximander's fragment is cosmological, it clearly reflects the inherited primitive view that nature is of a moral order.

How, then, does early modern man's engagement with nature differ from that of primitive man? The mythico-religious account that primitive man gives is imbued with imagination and reflects his intimate and intuitive connection with nature. The philosophico-scientific account of modern man strives to capture and narrate the whole in a manner that satisfies both reason and the imagination. Modern man must find a way to mediate his experience with nature, which has been rendered indirect through the exercise of reason. This need for mediation is the result of the shift from participant *in* to observer *of* nature, which carries with it a sense of distance and which contrasts with the immediacy of primitive man's experience.

This immediacy does not imply that nature consists of a series of uncoordinated sense-impressions for primitive man. Rather, it is a persistent whole, unified and organized through a collective mentality, which has a religious or mythical character. Cornford refers to this phenomenon as a "collective representation."[39] Collective representations are not the result of long accumulated scientific or philosophical inquiry,

---

[38] Unless otherwise indicated, all citations from the Presocratics are drawn from Kathleen Freeman's translation of Diels and will be identified by the fragment number, adopted from the fourth edition of Diels. *Ancilla to the Pre-Socratic Philosophers: A complete translation of the Fragments in Diels, "Fragmente der Vorsokratiker"* (Cambridge, MA: Harvard University Press, 1948).

[39] Cornford, borrowing from the French sociologist Lévy-Bruhl, further defines collective representations in *From Religion to Philosophy*: "They are common to the members of a given social group, within which they are transmitted from generation to generation; they are imposed upon the individuals, and awaken in them, as the case may be, feelings of respect, fear, adoration, etc., towards their objects. They do not depend for their existence upon the individual; not that they imply a collective subject distinct from the individuals composing the social group, but in that they present themselves with characters which cannot be accounted for merely by considering the individuals as such" (43-44).

nor are they dogma. They are a "common inherited scheme of conception, which is all around us and comes to us as naturally and unobjectionably as our native air, [which] is none the less imposed upon us and limits our intellectual movements in countless ways."[40] Collective representations differ from age to age in human history and are constantly undergoing changes, which are effected by the critical or intellectual efforts of a given period. When these representations are passed down, they are unchanged in the sense that they retain the marks of their collective origins. But the *way* in which they are received may radically differ from age to age. As Cornford points out, the religious notion of *moira* was for Hesiod a matter of *faith*, but for Anaximander a matter of *theory*.

In this way, the collective representation of nature that primitive man passes down to modern man becomes the primary "datum" of philosophy. Modern man cannot choose to ignore or abandon this representation. It has left an indelible mark on the view of nature as *physis*. Its religious or mythical character must be reconciled with the newfound demands of reason. While religion expresses itself in poetic symbols and in terms of mythical figures, philosophy aims at the language of abstraction. Modern man must thus mediate the collective representation of primitive man in a way that fulfills his speculative impulse and satisfies both his rational and his imaginative faculties. Modern man can accomplish this mediation by rendering the mythical account of his predecessors allegorical. This mediation allows for the formulation of a philosophical account while still acknowledging, and appropriating to some degree, the inherited primitive scheme. Philosophy accomplishes this appropriation by appealing to allegory.

Both of the allegorical traditions—interpretation and composition—move toward this end. By interpreting the mythico-religious accounts of primitive man, modern man is able to clarify and elucidate, from a rational perspective, the collective representation of the mythical tradition. Cornford asserts that the earliest philosophical speculations were nothing other than the analysis of religious, or pre-religious, mythical material; he claims that philosophy "does not create its new conceptual tools; it rather discovers them by ever subtler analysis and closer definition of the elements confused in its original datum."[41] By composing his own allegories, modern man implicitly and explicitly borrows elements from

---

[40] Ibid., 45.
[41] Ibid., 126.

the primitive scheme, but with the goal of creating an original philosophico-scientific account. In both of these practices, there is a sense of affinity or continuity with the mythical tradition, and the assumption that there is an opposition between muthos and logos is called into question.

The Shift from *Muthos* to *Logos*

The roots of the Western intellectual tradition can be traced back to a peculiar shift that occurred in ancient Greece from myth to philosophy.[42] Its fundamental importance for the development of humankind is widely recognized, but the details of this transition remain a subject of discussion. The shift in scholarship from maintaining the old opposition between *muthos* and *logos* to a more complex picture of their relationship has been well documented.[43] The long-standing view was that, sometime between the sixth and fourth centuries BCE, an intellectual revolution occurred in the ancient world. Faith in the tales of the creation of the world and its order, imbued with anthropomorphism, gradually gave way to a set of non-anthropomorphic and naturalistic explanations of the cosmos. The mythological accounts found in the poems of Homer and Hesiod were eventually replaced by the rational accounts set forth by the first philosophers, the Presocratics.

The terms employed in characterizing this shift, *muthos* and *logos*, are difficult to define, as is the nature of their relationship. The original meaning of *muthos* was "word" or "speech," in contrast to "deed" (*ergon*). It also denoted unspoken words or thoughts. Generally, it was used in reference to a story or narrative, though without any connotations of truth or falsity. Only in the fifth century did it come to suggest a fiction or

---

[42] The occurrence of this phenomenon in the East is also accounted for by various scholars: Karl Jaspers, in "The Axial Period" in *The Origin and Goal of History* (New Haven, CT: Yale University Press, 1965); Frankfort et al. in *Before Philosophy: The Intellectual Adventure of Early Man*; and tangentially by Paul Radin in *Primitive Man as Philosopher*. See also Mircea Eliade's *The Myth of the Eternal Return: Cosmos and History* and *Myth and Reality*, trans. Willard R. Trask (Long Grove, IL: Waveland Press, 1998).

[43] Some recent works surveying the question of *logos* and *muthos* include: Richard Buxton, ed., *From Myth to Reason? Studies in the Development of Greek Thought* (Oxford: Oxford University Press, 1999); Kathryn A. Morgan, *Myth and Philosophy from the Presocratics to Plato* (Cambridge: Cambridge University Press, 2000); and William Wians, ed., *Logos & Muthos: Philosophical Essays in Greek Literature* (Albany, NY: SUNY Press, 2010).

legend. At this point it is contrasted with *logos*, which by then was taken to imply something factual. *Logos* originally suggested a "reckoning" or an "account" of something. By the classical period, it came to have a wide variety of meanings: "proportion" or "measure"; "argument" or "reason"; "narrative" or "speech"; and finally, "a particular utterance" or "word."[44] Only in their secondary sense do the terms *muthos* and *logos* actually stand in opposition to one another. This fact suggests that the sharp distinction drawn between them in modern scholarship does not reflect their original usage in the ancient world, but rather satisfies the perceived need to clearly differentiate between the roles that myth and reason have played in human history.

When we turn from the individual meanings of the terms to the nature of their relationship, new difficulties emerge. First, it is problematic even to admit that there *is* a relationship of *muthos* to *logos*, despite the fact that the latter comes to supplant the former as the dominant mode of apprehending reality. The shift did not entail a "wholesale replacement" of myth by reason. Even those who argue for the development from a mythopoeic to a rational view of the world concede that mythical thinking never dies out completely.[45] Second, there are various problems that are associated with what has been called the "from . . . to . . ." thesis. There is the need to differentiate the developments that occur in disparate areas (philosophy, historiography, medicine, etc.) in light of their respective pasts and the traditions that they inherit and modify. There is also the need for sociological differentiation, which would determine the extent to which the common man was a part of these intellectual developments. Finally, there is the task of relating these developments in thought to changes in the practices current at that particular time. The biggest challenge involved in the "from . . . to . . ." thesis lies in explaining how this general process of intellectual development occurred, in all of its subtleties.[46]

This difficulty stems in part from the fact that modern scholars are inevitably left to consider myth from a post-mythic standpoint. They are

---

[44] *Greek-English Lexicon*, 9th edition, ed. H. G. Liddell and R. Scott (Oxford: Clarendon Press, 1996), s.vv. "μυθος" and "λογος."

[45] W. K. C. Guthrie, *Myth and Reason: Oration Delivered at the London School of Economics and Political Science on Friday, 12 December, 1952* (London: London School of Economics and Political Science, 1953), 7.

[46] See Richard Buxton, "Introduction" in *From Myth to Reason? Studies in the Development of Greek Thought*, ed. Richard Buxton (Oxford: Oxford University Press, 1999), 4-5.

prone to impose certain categories and distinctions on myth—e.g., the true versus the false, the objective versus the subjective, the real versus the imagined, and the universal versus the particular. These are products of the development in man's mode of apprehending both himself and the world. Although mythic consciousness has been said to possess its own logic and to deal with many of these concepts, it does so in a very different manner than philosophy. Roger Hinks asserts: "What distinguishes myth from logic is a difference in the mode of perceiving, and so of presenting, the same reality. The material upon which they work is the same: the nature of man and his relation to his environment. They differ in the place they assign to man in this environment, and consequently in their interpretation of his experience."[47] It is unclear whether the task of explaining the shift from *muthos* to *logos* can be facilitated by treating these two spheres as overlapping, to some extent, or by treating them as independent and even mutually exclusive modes of inquiry and expression.

Despite these difficulties, the fact that some sort of evolution occurred in the history of human consciousness cannot be ignored. The social sciences, particularly anthropology, have attempted, especially over the past two centuries, to provide "scientific" theories of myth. The modern discipline of philosophy has also engaged in this practice, though from a different standpoint. Philosophy is obliged to reflect upon the shift from *muthos* to *logos* because to do so is to inquire into its own origins. This inquiry into its own origins is precisely what distinguishes philosophy from all of the other sciences. It is the only discipline that takes its own nature to be a problem and thus an object of inquiry. The question of how and why philosophical thought emerges from the mythic mindset becomes even more pressing.

In response to this question, Karl Jaspers proposes a hypothesis in which the shift from *muthos* to *logos* is situated within the larger context of what he terms the "Axial Period." He describes this period as the process of gradual spiritualization that occurs from 800-200 BCE, centering around 500 BCE. Jaspers suggests that the Axial Period may serve as an empirical axis of world history, one that eclipses the differences between the pagan history of the ancients and the sacred history of the Judeo-Christian tradition. World history becomes rooted in the human

---

[47] Roger Hinks, *Myth and Allegory in Ancient Art* (London: The Warburg Institute, 1939), 7.

experience of history, which undergoes a radical shift in orientation during this time.

For Jaspers, the most distinctive feature of the Axial Period is that it is not an organic shift, but rather a spiritual shift. This increased spiritualization is evidenced by the appearance of the first prophets, philosophers, itinerant thinkers, and teachers in both the East and the West. While Jaspers acknowledges that the peaks of human potentiality are reached by only a handful of individuals, he insists that the whole of humanity takes a leap forward during this period. Man for the first time turns inward, but in doing so, he "becomes conscious of Being as a whole, of himself and his limitations. He experiences absoluteness in the depths of selfhood and in the lucidity of transcendence."[48]

Bruno Snell endeavors to explain the shift from *muthos* to *logos* by focusing on the nature of the early scientific thought that emerges from the break with myth. He inquires into the nature of comparison (*parabole*)—how it is employed and what function it serves—in both the mythical and philosophical frameworks. Snell's insight is that the Greek discovery of intellect can be traced back to how metaphor came to serve as the gateway to abstract thinking. He describes the process by which the Homeric similes, which captured only brief manifestations of life, were refashioned by Empedocles into comparisons that express a fact that is valid always and everywhere. According to Snell, the comparisons employed in myth were "chiefly a poetic way of increasing the pathos of a situation. Homer's similes, too, undoubtedly contribute to the creation of deep feeling, but their principal function is more direct. They constitute his only mechanism of describing the essence or the intensity of an event."[49] The philosophical formulation of metaphor as a logical analogy becomes the means by which man is able to achieve both the universality and necessity that myth lacks.

While Snell focuses on the subtleties of ancient Greek language to differentiate between the mythic and philosophical mentalities, Cornford looks to certain features of ancient Greek religion to clarify the true nature of the shift from *muthos* to *logos*. In so doing, he finds far more continuities than discontinuities between the mythical and philosophical modes of thought. As discussed above, he identifies certain conceptions—god, soul, destiny and law—that lie at the heart of primitive Greek religion

---

[48] Jaspers, 2.

[49] See Bruno Snell, "From Myth to Logic: The Role of the Comparison" in *The Discovery of Mind: The Greek Origins of European Thought*, 199-200. See also Chapter 2 herein for a more detailed discussion of this topic.

as forming the basis for early philosophical speculation. Although these conceptions are originally expressed in myth, ultimately they shape the first philosophers' understanding of nature as *physis*.

Cornford claims that while the supernatural character of these religious notions is gradually replaced by a metaphysical one, they otherwise remain the same: "The outward difference [between *muthos* and *logos*] only disguises an inward and substantial affinity between these two successive products of the same consciousness. The modes of thought that attain to clear definition and explicit statement in philosophy were already implicit in the unreasoned intuitions of mythology."[50] These observations suggest that the gulf between *muthos* and *logos* is perhaps not as wide as supposed and that philosophical speculation is not entirely separable from the mythic mode of thought.

Among the many modern scholars who investigate the Greek origins of philosophy, there are few who do not at least acknowledge the influence that myth has on early intellectual pursuits.[51] Even Aristotle, the most systematic of ancient thinkers, detected a certain affinity between myth and philosophy. He claims in the *Metaphysics* that the lover of myth (*philomuthos*) is in a sense a lover of wisdom (*philosophos*), for myths are composed of wonders, and it is owing to their wonder (*thauma*) that men first began and continue to philosophize. Aristotle connects the figures of the mythmaker and the philosopher by referring to their shared sense of wonder regarding the natural and supernatural worlds. The rapprochement of myth and philosophy is also the result of the inability to divorce reason from the imagination. Verene argues that the relationship between these two faculties is essential to understanding the real nature of philosophy and its relation to myth: "philosophical discourse as well as philosophy itself depends upon an aesthetic that cannot be overcome by reason, [and] there is a philosophical imaginary that necessarily accompanies

---

[50] Cornford, v.

[51] In addition to the works previously cited by Bruxton, Jaspers, Snell, and Cornford, see also F. M. Cornford, *Principium Sapientiae: The Origins of Greek Philosophical Thought* (Cambridge: Cambridge University Press, 1952); Lawrence J. Hatab, *Myth and Philosophy: A Contest of Truths* (La Salle, IL: Open Court, 1990); Marcel Detienne, *The Masters of Truth in Archaic Greece*, trans. Janet Lloyd (New York: Zone Books, 1996); Jean-Pierre Vernant, *The Origins of Greek Thought*, (Ithaca, NY: Cornell University Press, 1984); and Jean-Pierre Vernant, *Myth and Thought Among the Greeks*, trans. Janet Lloyd (New York: Zone Books, 2006).

philosophical rationality."[52] This aesthetic suggests that philosophy's origins lie in myth and that a definitive and unqualified shift from *muthos* to *logos* will never be realized. Philosophy will always have to strive to recover the imaginary element inherent in myth while simultaneously asserting its independence from myth.

Just as allegory served as the means by which the *muthos* of primitive man was transformed into the *logos* of modern man, it is also the means by which the relationship between these two modes of thought and discourse can be best understood. The earliest thinkers utilized both allegorical interpretation and composition to bridge any real or apparent gap between *muthos* and *logos*. They employed allegory, just as later thinkers would do, in an effort to connect the imaginary with the rational, a dynamic upon which philosophy itself depends. Although this dynamic can never be fully realized, it makes allegory and its attempt to render myth self-conscious an essential component of philosophy, its history, and its speculative project.

The chapters which follow explore three principal themes: that myth becomes self-conscious through allegory, that this sense of allegory entails a connecting of reason with the imagination, and that this connection makes possible the form of thought required by speculative philosophy. This conception of allegory could easily find its expression in more than one philosophical period. In fact, it might very well reveal itself as present, in some way or another, throughout the entire history of philosophy. Consider how Schelling describes the relationship of mythology to truth: "No single moment of mythology is the truth, only the process as a whole. Now, the various mythologies themselves are only different moments of the mythological process. . . . In the entirety of its successive moments, [mythology] is the way to truth and to this extent truth itself."[53] This view is reminiscent of the Hegelian perspective of philosophy and its relationship to truth. Allegory's development throughout the history of philosophy might be viewed as moments of a similar process. The truth identified with the whole that is sought by speculative philosophy is

---

[52] Verene, *Speculative Philosophy*, 56. Verene specifies that he understands "aesthetic" in the sense that it was originally defined by Alexander Baumgarten in 1735, as "the study of how things are cognized by means of the senses."

[53] As quoted in "Translator's Introduction," F.W.J. Schelling, *Historical-critical Introduction to the Philosophy of Mythology*, trans. Mason Richey and Markus Zisselsberger (Albany, NY: SUNY Press, 2007), xxi.

continually concealed and revealed through allegorical composition and interpretation. This process is ultimately constitutive of truth itself.

The central question is how this process *begins*—how allegory emerges out of the mythic tradition and how it is employed by the first philosophers in their attempts at rational speculation. This moment occurs at the onset of ancient Greek philosophy with the Presocratics, but it evolves over the course of classical antiquity, through Plato, the Hellenistic philosophers, and the Neoplatonists. Some of these later thinkers develop positions on allegory and begin to utilize it implicitly and explicitly in order to interpret the works of their predecessors as well as to formulate their own original philosophical insights. Allegory remains an important, even essential, feature of later philosophical thought, but by studying its emergence and development during the classical period, we are given a glimpse into its special significance for the origins of philosophy.

Studying allegory from this perspective is akin to studying philosophy itself, for in order to understand the nature of anything, it is necessary to understand its origins. In the case of both allegory and philosophy, these origins lie in myth. One question that immediately presents itself is how to overcome the opposition that is traditionally thought of as characterizing myth and philosophy. Again, consider how Schelling describes this relationship: "Nothing is more opposed than philosophy and mythology. But precisely in the opposition itself lies the definite challenge and the task of uncovering reason in just this which is apparently unreasonable, of uncovering meaning in just this which appears meaningless."[54] As mentioned above in the discussion of *muthos* and *logos*, these two modes of thought are not as opposed as once assumed. One commonality is their shared speculative impulse regarding the natural and supernatural worlds. This impulse results in accounts of very different sorts—one mythico-religious and one philosophico-scientific—and the question remains of how the latter both emerges from and reconciles itself with the former.

Allegory is the fundamental, though often implicit, background against which the transition from the mythical to the rational mindset occurs in early Greek thought. Allegory plays this role because it enables the first philosophers to grasp in thought and narrate in language the whole of reality, using both reason *and* the imagination. Because the task in

---

[54] Ibid., xi.

question is speculative in nature, it cannot be accomplished through the methods of critical reflection or analysis alone. This does not imply that other forms of philosophical discourse (e.g., treatise, dialogue, apology, confessional) are not legitimate or do not advance philosophical inquiry. Allegory differs from these other genres because, in many ways, it depends on myth and remains its closest counterpart once philosophical thought emerges from and supersedes the mythical. This closeness to myth gives allegory a special connection to the imagination. Through allegory, the imagination is put into service by reason so philosophical discourse may express both its imaginary and rational dimensions.

Allegory differs from myth in certain important respects. Though it shares myth's desire to express order in the world through a comprehensive narrative, allegory is more systematic and rational in its approach. Allegory "is always conscious; the writer knows what he is doing and why he is doing it. Myth cannot be conscious and invented, otherwise it would lose its sacred value, its quality of being divinely true."[55] Myth alone is able to achieve a narration of the whole in which all of the oppositions that characterize reality are encompassed. The faculty that accomplishes this is the imagination.

Once philosophy emerges, the oppositions that coalesce in myth become distinct in thought and must be mediated in language in order to render the corresponding account intelligible. The result is that, unlike myth, which *presents*, philosophy can only *represent* the whole. Alfred North Whitehead claims: "The creation of the world is the first unconscious act of speculative thought; and the first task of a self-conscious philosophy is to explain how it has been done."[56] Philosophy turns to allegory and its ability to "speak otherwise" in order to carry out this representation. The philosopher's reflections on the truths expressed obliquely in the mythic narrative give rise to the tradition of allegorical interpretation. The philosopher's attempt to narrate the whole in other speech yields the tradition of allegorical composition.

---

55 Gay Clifford, *The Transformations of Allegory* (London: Routledge & Kegan Paul Ltd,, 1974), 66.
56 Alfred North Whitehead, *Aims of Education and Other Essays* (New York: The Free Press, 1967), 164.

Chapter 2
The Presocratics and the Beginnings of Allegory

> Though philosophy means death to the old gods, it is itself religion;
> and the seeds it has sown now thrive in the new theogony.
>
> Werner Jaeger, *The Theology of the Early Greek Philosophers*

Historical and Theoretical Considerations

The Presocratics are the natural starting point for a discussion on the role that allegory plays in the shift from mythical to rational thought and the origins of philosophy. These early Greek thinkers are the direct heirs of Homer and Hesiod and the first real critics of the poetic tradition. Their position in the history of philosophy is unique insofar as they straddle both sides of the so-called divide between *muthos* and *logos*. They also foreshadow the speculative impulse that characterizes modern man. We see in their extant fragments—occasionally even those attributed to the same author—both a critique and a defense of mythical consciousness. In these instances, we can detect in their writings, and in their philosophy as a whole, a certain kind of tension. There is the impulse to relinquish the older and well-established worldview of the poets in favor of a new and radical understanding of physical and, in some cases, metaphysical reality, but there is also an earnest attempt to incorporate the poetic worldview into their philosophical discourse. The latter tendency will manifest itself in the Presocratic project of interpretation of the poets as well as in the composition of their own allegorical works.

The peculiar position occupied by the Presocratics is in part overlooked because of certain misconceptions that arise when considering them from a modern standpoint. One challenge comes simply from referring to these thinkers as "Presocratics," a name that situates them exclusively in relation to Plato's Socrates. The term first became current in English after Hermann Diels published his seminal work on early Greek philosophy, *Die Fragmente der Vorsokratiker* in 1903. Taken in a strict chronological sense, this appellation is inaccurate in that several of the later Presocratics, particularly the Sophists of the fourth and fifth centuries, were contemporaries of both Socrates and Plato. This usage of the term has also come to distinguish the natural philosophy of these early Greek thinkers from the moral philosophy of Socrates. But many of the

Presocratic thinkers delved into the realms of metaphysics, epistemology, and ethics, and often overlooked cosmological concerns in pursuit of these inquiries. The term also suggests that the Presocratics are somehow inferior to Socrates and Plato and that their import only lies in their role as predecessors. It implies that their philosophical speculations were too archaic or naïve to stand alone and can be measured only in terms of the more sophisticated schools of thought that followed them.

Another challenge comes from ascribing the title "philosopher" to the Presocratics because of the many connotations that this term has come to have. It suggests that these individuals were intellectual theorists and overlooks the breadth and variety of their practical concerns. Heraclitus uses the term in one of the fragments attributed to him by Clement, although not necessarily in reference to himself: "Men who are lovers of wisdom must be inquirers into very many things indeed" (fr. 35). But the word he uses (*philosophos*) does not yet have the technical sense it acquires in Plato and Aristotle. It suggests that the Presocratics thought of themselves as inquirers into a vast range of topics—from physics and psychology to epistemology and metaphysics.

Although he left no writings, Pythagoras is purportedly the only one of the early Greek thinkers who identified himself as a philosopher. Whether or not this is historically accurate, it cannot be denied that he was the first, and perhaps the only, Presocratic to espouse and teach philosophy as a *way of life*, including certain dietary restrictions, religious rituals, and purification practices. Some of these ideas, particularly the Pythagorean teachings on the soul and its afterlife, become an integral part of both Socratic and Platonic philosophy. Yet, it is still anachronistic to think of the Presocratics as "philosophers" in any modern sense.

To classify the Presocratics as philosophers simply in order to distinguish them from the archaic poets is misleading. It implies the largely non-philosophical character of the early Greek poets and the largely non-poetical character of the early Greek philosophers. This distinction cannot be based on their medium of discourse, as several of the Presocratics wrote in verse. Moreover, there are certain aspects of archaic poetry that anticipate the philosophical enterprise. It is true that the Presocratics conceived of themselves as undertaking an intellectual pursuit that was distinct in nature from the poets and the historical writers who were their predecessors and contemporaries. While they broke with the poetic tradition in many respects, the view that the musings of these first philosophers were devoid of poetic influence is subject to question.

Andrea Nightingale suggests that a better way of thinking about these individuals and their role in archaic Greek culture begins with a consideration of how wisdom (*sophia*) was conceived in the sixth and fifth centuries. The term "wise men" (*sophoi*), she argues, is a more accurate name for the Presocratic philosophers because of its wide range of application, which included poets, prophets, doctors, statesmen, astronomers, scientists, historians, inventors, and various kinds of artisans.[1] The question then becomes what is required to identify a certain set of *sophoi* as philosophers. A partial response to this question is that the *sophoi* during this period sought to "perform wisdom" by displaying or enacting it in a public context. Nightingale is careful not to equate this type of performance with that of the traditional poets, who enjoyed a much greater popularity in Greek culture. Her point is that it was necessary for the early Greek thinkers to create their own audiences in order to disseminate their philosophical ideas to a non-specialized sector of Greek society. If we approach our study of the Presocratics with some caution, if we think of them not as philosophers in any modern sense of the word, but rather as ambitious individuals staking a claim to *sophia* as it was conceived in ancient Greece at the time, then we can hope to get a better understanding of their unique role as inheritors of the poetic tradition and as pioneers of philosophical speculation.

These figures occupied a revolutionary period in intellectual history. The Presocratic era was marked by thinkers who were expounding theories that were profoundly innovative and experimental. More remarkably, as Nightingale points out, "these individuals were not only practicing theoretical speculation but were also engaged in political, poetic, salvific and theological projects akin to those of nonphilosophical *sophoi* of the [Presocratic] period."[2] While there is some cohesion to these thinkers and their intellectual endeavors, a number of distinct movements developed over the course of the sixth and fifth centuries, which we now classify chronologically and geographically as: the Ionians, Pythagoreans, Eleatics, pluralists, atomists, and the Sophists. Xenophanes and Heraclitus do not fit neatly into this classification, but are nonetheless crucial figures in the movement. All of these thinkers sought to answer one or more of the following fundamental and interrelated questions: the *ontological*

---

[1] Andrea Wilson Nightingale, "The Philosophers in Archaic Greek Culture," in *The Cambridge Companion to Archaic Greece*, ed. H. A. Shapiro (Cambridge: Cambridge University Press, 2007), 173.

[2] Ibid., 177.

(What is the first principle, or *arche*, of existence?); the *cosmological* (How does this principle allow for change to occur?); the *epistemological* (How can we validate our knowledge of Being and becoming?); and the *ethical* (What is man's relation to his human counterparts and to the divine?).

Despite the modern practice of classifying the early Greek thinkers based on geography, chronology, or even overlapping intellectual concerns, differences in their methodologies and interests should not be overlooked. While the period is sometimes broken down into a series of schools of thought, this classification should not be understood as "schools" in the literal sense of Plato's Academy or Aristotle's Lyceum. The feature that best characterizes the Presocratics is the variety of their philosophical pursuits. The Ionian thinkers—Thales, Anaximander, and Anaximenes—were dominated by an interest in the physical nature of the cosmos. Pythagoras and his followers abandoned this approach and moved from an inquiry into the physical *nature* of the cosmos to a study of its *form*.

Xenophanes and Heraclitus focused on theological issues and introduced the important epistemological question of how human knowledge is not only possible, but how it can be certain. Parmenides and the Eleatics rejected the theories of their predecessors and pursued a strictly metaphysical investigation into the nature of Being. The pluralists and atomists, each in their own way, attempted to reconcile the Eleatic principle of Being with the obvious fact of plurality and change in nature. The Sophists turned their attention to the moral and social issues that were of increasing importance in Greek society.

It should be noted that the literary techniques employed by the Presocratics were as varied as their philosophical interests. It would be impossible to construct a complete picture of their literary methodology because only limited sources are available. From the extant fragments and testimonia, however, we do know that these early thinkers wrote in both prose and verse. Among the Ionians, Anaximander and Anaximenes are both thought to have written books (in prose), but the former apparently utilized "rather poetical terminology" compared with the "simple and unsuperfluous" language of the latter.[3] Xenophanes wrote exclusively in verse and was said to have composed both philosophical and sympotic

---

[3] G. S. Kirk, J. E. Raven, and M. Schofield, eds., *The Presocratic Philosophers*, 2nd ed. (Cambridge: Cambridge University Press, 1983), 144.

poems. What remains of Heraclitus's writings takes the form of carefully formulated opinions, often under the guise of riddles.

As mentioned above, it is generally accepted that Pythagoras wrote nothing, while Parmenides is credited with one of the longest extant works among the early Presocratics—a metaphysical poem in the traditional epic form of hexameter verse. Later Eleatics, however, returned to prose. Zeno is typically associated with the technique of antinomy or paradox and Melissus with the practice of deductive argumentation. Of the pluralists, Empedocles wrote in hexameter verse, while Anaxagoras and the atomists, Leucippus and Democritus, all wrote in prose. The Sophists of the fifth century introduced new techniques in their writings, including argumentative strategies, display speeches, parody, and poetic exegesis.

The various literary forms employed by the Presocratics provide insight into the role that these early thinkers play in the advent of allegory. Two figures in particular—Pherecydes of Syros and Theagenes of Rhegium—are important in this respect, although they might be considered peripheral to the Presocratic period. Also of great importance is the Derveni papyrus, an allegorical commentary on an Orphic poem, discovered only recently, composed sometime during the fifth century. Although the author of the commentary is unknown, his outlook is philosophical and echoes the physical systems of Anaxagoras and the atomists. Pherecydes, Theagenes, and the author of the Derveni papyrus are all relevant, alongside the more prominent Presocratics, to a discussion of how allegory emerges as a way of mediating between the mythical tradition and the early Greek philosophical project.

Even those Presocratic philosophers who wrote strictly in prose or who were not explicitly associated with the beginnings of Greek allegory were not immune to poetic influences. As Frankfort points out, "the doctrines of the early Greek philosophers [were] not couched in the language of detached and systematic reflection. Their sayings sound rather like inspired oracles."[4] Heraclitus immediately comes to mind, but this could also apply to thinkers such as Parmenides, who invokes a divine source (the goddess) at the beginning of *On Nature*, which is reminiscent of Homer's and Hesiod's invocation of the Muses in their own poems. This tendency of the Presocratics to incorporate mythical elements into their philosophical discourse is not so surprising given their proximity, in both time and culture, to the archaic poets. Like Hesiod, a Boeotian farmer, the

---

[4] Frankfort et al., 251.

early Greek thinkers were not professional seers, yet they made it their vocation to investigate the natural world and disseminate their theories. They also shared with their predecessors, and particularly Hesiod, a concern for origins; but for the Presocratics, the *arche* assumed a radically new character because they sought to understand it independently of myth.

What Frankfort calls the "speculative courage" of these early thinkers and the "preposterous boldness" of their assumption (i.e., that a single order underlies the chaos of our perceptions and that we can understand that order) may explain their receptivity to poetic influence.[5] They are perhaps the best example of philosophers in the sense that Aristotle intended when he claimed that "all philosophy begins in wonder," since that is most certainly the feeling evoked by their intuitive yet intelligible grasp of the whole. While they might have adopted a critical attitude and rejected the poets' appeal to external authority in validating their claims, we nevertheless find in certain Presocratic writings gaps in rational explanation, breaks in the connection between theory and evidence, and even the occasional appeal to the Muses. We would be incorrect in asserting that the Presocratics signaled a complete and clean break with the mythical tradition. An examination of their place in the shift from *muthos* to *logos*, however, will allow us to move from a *poetic influence* on the Presocratics to a Presocratics *poetics*.

It is commonly assumed that in undertaking an investigation of the cosmos from a scientific perspective, the early Greek thinkers were implicitly and explicitly separating themselves from the poetic worldview of the mythical age. This view is in many ways true, but it risks the same oversimplification of the *muthos-logos* distinction, which was discussed earlier.[6] The Presocratics broke with the mythic tradition in that they reconceived the origins and nature of the world primarily through the lens of reason. Blind acceptance of the external authority of the poets gave way to reliance upon the individual human intellect and, particularly, the ability to posit an *arche* and argue for its validity using naturalistic explanations and deductive reasoning. This change in viewpoint is indeed a significant moment in the birth of philosophy. Previously, myth was the only source of wisdom, and its validity resided not only in the authority of the divinely inspired poets, but also in its acceptance by the faithful. Beginning with the Presocratics, however, myth becomes subject to justification by the

---

[5] Ibid., 251-52.
[6] See Chapter 1 herein for a more detailed discussion of this shift.

critical. This signals, according to Frankfort, a shift of the problems of man in nature from the realm of faith and poetic intuition to the intellectual sphere.[7]

Even more remarkable than this shift is the fact that it was recognized and described relatively soon after it occurred. Plato does this, albeit indirectly, in his dialogues when he contrasts the natures of *muthos* and *logos*. He does not distinguish sharply between poets and philosophers among his predecessors nor does he explicitly identify the Presocratics as pivotal figures in the transition from *muthos* to *logos*. In the *Protagoras*, Plato has Protagoras argue that the ancient poets were actually Sophists in disguise: "Now, I maintain that the sophist's art is an ancient one, but that the men who practiced it in ancient times, fearing the odium attached to it, disguised it, masking it sometimes as poetry, as Homer and Hesiod and Simonides did" (316d-e).

Aristotle was the first author to provide the terminology that reinforces the sharp division between the *muthos*-seeking poets and the *logos*-seeking Presocratics. He contrasts them in the first chapter of the *Poetics*, when he asserts: "Homer and Empedocles, however, have really nothing in common apart from their metre; so that, if one is to be called a poet, the other should be termed a physicist rather than a poet" (1447b).[8] Aristotle is distinguishing between two groups of thinkers: the *theologoi* and the *phusikoi*.[9] The former denoted the ancient storytellers and poets who composed and recited myths about heroes and gods. They were imitators, and any views about the nature of the world that might be extracted from their stories and poems could be considered incidental, obscure, and philosophically insignificant. The *phusikoi* were the natural philosophers who undertook the first truly scientific investigation of the physical world.

Even though the theories of the Presocratics were rudimentary and deficient in light of later ones, particularly those that Aristotle himself developed, they are philosophically significant and worth studying. At the very least, the *phusikoi* shared in Aristotle's commitment to explain the

---

[7] Frankfort et al., 251.

[8] Unless otherwise indicated, all citations from Aristotle's works are drawn from Richard McKeon, ed., *The Basic Works of Aristotle* (New York: Modern Library, 2001).

[9] For one of many instances of this distinction, see *Metaphysics* XII.6, where Aristotle writes: "Yet if we follow the theologians (*theologoi*) who generate the world from night, or the natural philosophers (*phusikoi*) who say that 'all things were together,' the same impossible result ensues" (1071b).

world in terms of its own inherent principles. This approach contrasts with the method of the *theologoi*, who posited the gods as external causes of the world, thereby rendering cosmology inseparable from theogony.

In distinguishing the natural philosophers from the poetic theologians, Aristotle offers the first attempt to systematize and analyze the doctrine of his predecessors; he can thus be identified as the first historian of philosophy. His accounts of the views of the Presocratics in the *Physics* and *Metaphysics* provide significant evidence of their ideas, which would have otherwise risked obscurity through lack of transmission. The way in which Aristotle classifies these thinkers is somewhat arbitrary. He deems certain thinkers *phusikoi* only because they appear to have grasped one of his four causes and articulated it in a relatively clear manner. In fact, all of the Presocratics identified the first principles of the cosmos as divine in nature. Thales's water, Anaximander's *apeiron*, Anaximenes's *aer*, Heraclitus's *logos,* and Anaxagoras' *Nous* depart from the poetic conception of the gods as anthropomorphic deities, but they retain an element of the divine. For these early Greek thinkers, *phusis* was not at odds with divinity. As Nightingale points out, Aristotle's distinction is misleading, since "it privileges the materialist aspects of [Presocratic] cosmologies, while downplaying if not occluding their radical theories of divine essence."[10]

Aristotle's classification of his predecessors is nevertheless in harmony with his other views regarding the true nature of poetry, particularly his discussion of *poiesis, praxis,* and *theoria* in the *Nicomachean Ethics*. There, *poiesis* refers to production, the purposeful bringing into being of something distinct from its human producer; *praxis* refers to human activity in the temporal and contingent realm; and *theoria* refers to contemplation of objects in the eternal and unchanging realm. Aristotle, like Plato, considers poetry as a kind of making or producing, one that involves imitation (*mimesis*). The product of this making is the story (*muthos*). But just as *poiesis* is inferior to *theoria* in its activity, its end or what it produces, i.e., myths or stories, is only provisionally satisfying to the philosopher, who must look beyond them to find the eternal and unchanging objects of contemplation.

The distinction between the *theologoi* and the *phusikoi* is taken up by Aristotle's student, Theophrastus (c. 371-c. 287) in his collection of physical doctrines of the early Greek thinkers. Theophrastus's work served

---

[10] Nightingale, 173.

as the basis upon which all ancient, and ultimately modern, discussions of the Presocratics were constructed. His *Phusikon doxai* ("Physical Tenets"), after undergoing various revisions, abridgments, and expansions, was used by later Greek and Roman schools, as well as by the Church Fathers and other writers.[11] In light of this fact, it is easy to see how Aristotle's distinction between the poets and the first philosophers becomes more far-reaching over time. The difference between the so-called *theologoi* and the *phusikoi* becomes not simply one of verse over prose, but comes to involve more significant oppositions—between myth and reason, tradition and innovation, religion and science, community and individual, and error and truth. An entire tradition of scholarship on the Presocratics has been built upon divorcing them from their poet predecessors. The influence of the poets on them has been largely overlooked.

Philosophical Anticipations in Archaic Poetry

The assumption that the Presocratics represented a complete break with the mythical worldview is overdrawn. The early Greek thinkers did make efforts to distance themselves from certain aspects of the poetic tradition and its approach to reality. Their critique and abandonment of Homer's and Hesiod's depiction of the gods provide some evidence for this position. The world of the ancient poets was saturated with deities and was entirely subject to their capricious intervention; the early Greek thinkers rejected this account and viewed the world as naturally ordered, inherently intelligible, and not subject to supra-natural intervention.

G. S. Kirk points out that the Presocratics were slow to reject the symbols and imagery employed by the poets, in part because their use of personification had not been completely anti-rational. He suggests: "The division of the world between a plurality of deities and daimons with different properties and powers was in itself a valuable act of classification."[12] Even Heraclitus, a harsh critic of the poets, occasionally reinterpreted the functions and values of these symbols rather than wholly abandoning them. Given their gradual and sometimes ambivalent progress from *muthos* to *logos*, it would be inaccurate to speak of the absolute

---

[11] Jaap Mansfeld, "Sources," in *The Cambridge Companion to Early Greek Philosophy*, ed. A.A. Long (Cambridge: Cambridge University Press, 1999), 23.

[12] Kirk et al., 72.

rationality of the Presocratic philosophers. It would also be inaccurate to attribute a sheer irrationality to the ancient poets.

One feature of the mythical tradition that has often been considered irrational is its epistemology, or its lack thereof. The archaic poets' view of knowledge was heavily influenced by the role they believed the gods played in human affairs in general. Homer was critiqued by some of the early Greek thinkers, especially Xenophanes and Heraclitus, not only because of his anthropomorphic depiction of the gods but also because he implied that human knowledge was utterly dependent on the gods for its validity. This view of the gods is expressed, directly and indirectly, at various points in the *Iliad* and *Odyssey*, but its most classic expression is in Homer's appeal to the Muses.

In Book II of the *Iliad*, Homer invokes the Muses for a second time prior to his recounting of the catalogue of ships: "And now, O Muses, dwellers in the mansions of Olympus, tell me—for you are goddesses and are in all places so that you see all things, while we know nothing but by report" (*Il.* 2.485-86).[13] The Presocratics rejected the poetic appeal to external and divine authority because of their growing confidence in man's own intellectual abilities. While they certainly conceived of human knowledge as limited and imperfect, they sought to emancipate it from the domain of the gods. The possibility of an archaic, specifically Homeric, epistemology is nevertheless of some importance, particularly because it suggests one of the many ways in which archaic poetry anticipated later aspects of philosophical inquiry.

There is general agreement that the Homeric poems treated knowledge as essentially a matter of sense perception and specifically linked it to the faculty of sight. To know (*noein*) something is to have acquired it by direct experience, namely, by seeing it. Homer's appeal to the Muses makes explicit this connection between knowledge and vision—the goddesses possess knowledge of things past, present, and future because they see *all* things. Furthermore, this view of knowledge highlights the fact that even for the gods, and not just for humans, knowledge is derived primarily through sense-experience. Indeed, Homer consistently credits both gods and mortals with discovering the truth by means of direct observation of events.

---

[13] Unless otherwise indicated, all citations are drawn from *The Iliad of Homer*, trans. Samuel Butler, (Cambridge: Cambridge University Press, 1898).

There is, however, a great difference in the quantity and quality of the knowledge that is available to each group based on their respective capacities. The Muses are omnipresent, so their account of things is more accurate and more complete than any mortal could ever hope to offer. Their task, as daughters of Memory (*Mnemosyne*), is to "enlarge the recollection of the poet" so that he might sing of things of which he has little or no direct experience.[14] These poets are chosen and favored by the gods, and it is due to this fact alone that they may lay claim to knowledge of things both human and divine. The gods are credited with supplying reliable information to humans through dreams, omens, portents, and oracles. They also seem to privilege certain individuals by endowing them with the ability to know more than what is afforded the average mortal; this ability is demonstrated through the figures of prophets, seers, and simply those individuals, such as heroes, who are favored by the gods.

The close connection between knowledge and sense-experience in Homer has led some to argue that there is no real concept of *knowledge* that can form the basis of an archaic epistemology, but rather only a concept of *knowledge by personal experience*. Others challenge this view, arguing that there is evidence in both the *Odyssey* and the *Iliad* that contradicts it. Edward Hussey sketches four instances in which the thesis limiting archaic knowledge to direct experience cannot be sustained. The first is that the gods and divinely privileged seers are said to know about the future, which cannot be derived from personal experience. The second is that even non-privileged human beings occasionally make claims to know about the future, and they are not treated as mad for doing so. The third is that other human beings make claims to know about things that they have not directly experienced, whether in the present or near past, or about general truths, and this occurs without controversy. The fourth is that throughout the epics, there is an assumed background knowledge of basic truths about the general nature and history of the world that is enjoyed by both the gods and human beings.[15] These instances suggest that while the identification of knowledge and vision in Homeric epic holds true in general, there may be other, subtler forms of knowing that constitute, or at least contribute toward, a so-called archaic epistemology.

---

[14] See Bruno Snell, *The Discovery of the Mind*, 136-38.

[15] See Edward Hussey, "The beginnings of epistemology: from Homer to Philolaus" in *Companions to Ancient Thought 1: Epistemology*, ed. Stephen Everson (Cambridge: Cambridge University Press, 1990), 13. See in particular footnotes 7, 8, and 9 for textual evidence supporting these instances.

These other forms of knowing are elaborated by J. H. Lesher in his discussion of archaic structures of knowledge in Homer. He argues that the early Greek poets often spoke in different ways about human knowledge, and this extended beyond the strict identification of knowing with seeing. According to Lesher: "A person might appropriately assert *autos oida*—'I know for myself'—on the basis of what he or she had directly observed; another might claim to have learned the truth from a reliable source; while a third might make a claim to knowledge on the basis of a trial or testing process."[16] Citing passages from both the *Iliad* and *Odyssey*, Lesher proposes three Homeric ways of knowing: through observation, testimony, or trial. The view that an archaic conception of knowledge might be more complex than first imagined is also advanced by Kirk, who attributes a sort of practical wisdom to the epic hero of Homer's work: "The Homeric conception of Odysseus . . . is of a man capable, in most ways at least, of philosophy—distinguished not so much by 'cunning' as by the power of analyzing complex circumstances and making rational choices as a result."[17] There seems to be general agreement about a logical and psychological refinement present in the poetry of Homer that renders an archaic epistemology not only possible but also far less primitive than once assumed.

Setting aside the subtleties of the Homeric position, the "developmentalist view" of how the early Greeks conceived of human knowledge contends that knowing and the various forms of experience with which it is associated in Homer continue to be expressed by various Presocratic thinkers. Heraclitus seems to echo the Homeric view of knowledge when he writes: "Those things of which there is sight, hearing, knowledge: these are what I honour most" (fr. 55) and "Human nature has no power of understanding; but the divine nature has it" (fr. 78). Xenophanes claims: "And as for certain truth, no man has seen it, nor will there ever be a man who knows about the gods and about all the things I mention" (fr. 34). These fragments might be taken as revealing a continuity with the poets' view of human knowledge; at the very least, they support the idea that the mythical worldview was not as irrational as generally assumed.

---

[16] J. H. Lesher, "Archaic Knowledge," in *Logos and Muthos*, ed. William Wians (Albany, NY: SUNY Press, 2009), 17. See also, J. H. Lesher, "Perceiving and Knowing in the 'Iliad' and 'Odyssey'," *Phronesis* 26 (1981): 2-24.

[17] Kirk et al., 73.

This continuity is also demonstrated in relation to another feature of Homer's epistemology, i.e., the epic simile. The epic simile is a comparison, often rather elaborate in both its form and length, between two unlike objects. It is more prestigious than the simple simile insofar as it is employed to intensify the heroic stature of the text. The epic simile, as a species of metaphor, is considered in some detail by Bruno Snell in his discussion of the role of comparison in the shift from myth to logic. He describes Homer's use of these similes as *necessary* insofar as they are "indispensable for the description of all intellectual and spiritual phenomena."[18] In other words, they serve as his only means for describing the essence of a person, thing, or event.

Since Homeric thought and language was not sufficiently abstract, there is a certain concreteness associated with them. While metaphor is by definition figurative, the Homeric simile is almost literal in the sense that it describes "a slice of life in motion," and is accordingly always based on a verb, rather than an adjective.[19] For instance, Homer writes: "As when some mighty wave that thunders on the beach when the west wind has lashed it into fury . . . even so did the serried phalanxes of the Danaans march steadfastly into battle" (*Il.* 4.21ff). According to Snell, the human action described here *requires* the comparison in order to achieve its full expression, rather than to fulfill the abstract *tertium comparationis* of the adjectival metaphor.[20]

Another way of expressing this is that Homeric similes are more metaphysical in nature than epistemological. They seek to reveal the essence or nature of a thing by reading its qualities into another thing; this secondary thing, in turn, sheds light on the original thing. In this way, these similes reveal a fundamental condition of the primitive or mythic mindset—that "human behavior is made clear only through reference to something else which is in turn explained by analogy with human behavior" or that "man must listen to an echo of himself before he may hear or know himself."[21] The relationship between the two elements in an epic simile is more direct or concrete, and is in keeping with how primitive man engages with nature. The relationship between the elements in the

---

[18] Snell, 198.
[19] Verene, *Speculative Philosophy*, 113. See also Snell's discussion of adjectival versus verbal metaphors, 194ff.
[20] Snell, 200.
[21] Ibid., 200-201.

adjectival metaphor—and by extension, allegory—is indirect and abstract. This relationship reflects how modern man relates to and understands reality once philosophical thought has superseded mythical thought.

The archaic mode of comparison through the epic simile is both adopted and modified by later Presocratic thinkers. Snell cites Empedocles as foremost in formulating his comparisons on the pattern of the Homeric similes, but other early Greek thinkers also demonstrate this same tendency. Consider the following fragments of Anaximander and Anaximenes: "[The Earth is like] a stone column" (fr. 5) and "[The sun is broad] like a leaf (fr. 2a)." Simple as they are, these fragments illustrate a shift from the verbal similes employed by Homer to the adjectival metaphors employed by the Presocratics, in which the comparison refers to a resemblance or a property.

Heraclitus's writings are suggestive of this shift to a greater degree than his Ionian predecessors, but the specific nature of his reflections are difficult to classify because of the contradictions they embody. His aphorisms seek to uncover a universal identity in the elements he compares, but this is often done by means of opposing them, evidenced by the fragment, "harmony consists of opposing tension, like that of the bow and the lyre" (fr. 51). While they might not possess the metaphysical necessity of the epic similes, these comparisons are valuable because they point to the type of abstraction required by a philosophical rather than an archaic epistemology. More generally, they illustrate the shift that occurs during this period from the mythico-religious mode of thought of the archaic poets to the philosophico-scientific modes of the early Greek thinkers.

It is Empedocles who really exemplifies how the implicitness of an archaic epistemology is made explicit by the Presocratics. Snell appeals to the following fragment of Empedocles to examine how this shift occurs: "As when a man, thinking to make an excursion through a stormy night, prepares a lantern, a flame of burning fire, fitting lantern-plates to keep out every sort of winds, and these plates disperse the breath of the blowing winds; but the light leaps out through them, in so far as it is finer, and shines across the threshold with unwearying beams: so at that time did the aboriginal Fire, confined in membranes and in fine tissues, hide itself in the round pupils; and these were pierced throughout with marvellous passages" (fr. 84).

There are several differences between the epic simile and its Presocratic counterpart. The first, rather superficial, difference is that

Empedocles "limits his images to the area of the skills and techniques, while Homer takes most of his similes from the sphere of animals, nature, and the life of the herdsmen, the peasants and the fishermen."[22] The second difference has already been noted: Homer's verbal similes concern themselves with actions, with capturing brief manifestations of life. Empedocles seeks to describe and explain more permanent, enduring operations; for instance, how vision works in the fragment cited above. Snell's analysis gives rise to the most important difference between the two types of comparison. The Homeric simile remains in the realm of the particular and the concrete while the Presocratic metaphor seeks to express the universal and general nature of the things being compared. This difference is both the starting point and the end point of the abstract thinking that lies at the heart of the shift from myth to logic.

As the other great educator of archaic Greek society, Hesiod provides further examples of how archaic poetry anticipated some of the rational tenets that the Presocratics would ultimately adopt in their own philosophical speculations. Although he lived only a generation or so later than Homer, Hesiod represented a new attempt at the systematizing of ancient myths. The order of the world and its development found only occasional expression in Homer's *Iliad* and *Odyssey*. The systematizing of myths became the focus of both Hesiod's *Theogony* and *Works and Days*. As Kirk points out, the plan of compiling a systematic cosmogony and theogony presupposed a comprehensive view of the world, including its organization, its principle of operation, and man's part within it.[23] A. A. Long refers to this project as "giving an account of all things" and characterizes it as the attempt "to give a universalist account, to show what the 'all' or the universe is like, to take everything—the world as a whole—as the subject of inquiry."[24] This type of inquiry describes the intellectual pursuit of the early Greek philosophers, yet Hesiod undertook a similar project, albeit through the language of myths. For this reason, Hesiod has sometimes been treated as one of the first Presocratic philosophers, or at least as their closest predecessor in chronology and in spirit.

---

[22] Ibid., 214.

[23] Kirk et al., 73.

[24] A. A. Long, "The scope of early Greek philosophy" in *The Cambridge Companion to Early Greek Philosophy*, ed. A. A. Long (Cambridge: Cambridge University Press, 1999), 10.

Heraclitus groups Hesiod together with three other early Greek thinkers in this fragment: "Much learning does not teach one to have intelligence; for it would have taught Hesiod and Pythagoras, and again, Xenophanes and Hecataeus" (fr. 40). Heraclitus is not associating the archaic poet with the Presocratics in a positive sense, but is differentiating his own thought from the "polymathy" inherent in Hesiod's poetry, Hecataeus's history, and Xenophanes's and Pythagoras's respective philosophies. The multiplicity that contaminates their accounts obscures Heraclitus's central truth, which he expresses in the following fragment: "When you have listened, not to me but to the Law (*Logos*), it is wise to agree that *all things are one*" (fr. 50; italics mine). The earlier fragment reveals that Hesiod was occasionally thought of as blurring the line between the archaic poets and the early philosophers.

Long enumerates five ways in which the Presocratic project of giving an account of all things differed from that of Hesiod. The early Greek philosophers' accounts were, or sought to be: (1) explanatory and systematic in the sense of *logos* over *muthos*; (2) coherent and argumentative in regard to both man's empirical observations and conceptual abilities; (3) transformative, in order to awaken people from their individual delusions; (4) educationally provocative, in contrast to the blind acceptance by the poets' audiences; and (5) critical and unconventional, even if this repudiated the received wisdom of the poets.[25] These criteria make it difficult to bridge the gap that lies between Hesiod's narration of the whole and later Presocratic accounts. They reveal how the early Greek philosophers strove to replace cosmogony, with its strong irrational elements, with cosmology, while still exhibiting the speculative concerns of their predecessors.

In terms of his contribution to an archaic epistemology, Hesiod exhibits some important differences from the Homeric contribution. Although he appeals to the authority of the Muses in both his *Theogony* and *Works and Days*, he has a different conception of his relation to them. In his lengthy invocation of the Muses at the beginning of the *Theogony*, he has the Muses speak for the first time: "Shepherds of the wilderness, wretched things of shame, mere bellies, we know how to speak many false things as though they were true; but we know, when we will, to utter true

---

[25] Ibid., 13.

things" (*Theog.* 26-28).²⁶ Just prior to the invocation, he names himself as the poet to whom the Muses taught their song. With this use of the first-person pronoun, Hesiod creates an identity for himself as poet. As such, he occupies an intermediary role between those who have not been graced by the Muses and the gods themselves. Snell says: "Hesiod looks upon himself as a special type of man, and his truth is of a special perfection. He is subjective in the sense that he has his own understanding of what objective truth is. His knowledge, *in fine*, stands half way between the divine knowledge of the Muses and the human knowledge of the fools."²⁷

Noteworthy in Hesiod's invocation is the apparent duplicity that he attributes to the Muses, present in neither the invocation of *Works and Days* nor anywhere in the Homeric epics. Why does Hesiod describe the Muses as speaking of both true *and* false things? One common interpretation is that Hesiod is referring in these lines to those singers who are inferior to him and whose songs do not reveal the same degree of truthfulness as his own.²⁸ In this case, the "false things" (*pseuda*) have a negative sense and refer to the deceptions of a poetry that Hesiod contrasts with his own. Accordingly, the Muses' declaration could be understood as a polemic directed at Homer or even at heroic epic in general. Another interpretation is that the Muses' two modes reflect the extent of their knowledge, which is an unqualified and complete reflection of reality. The whole or complete speech of the Muses would necessarily include both truth and falsity just as the whole of reality contains both what is positive and negative.²⁹

Setting aside the literary criticism it has engendered, this passage might also be taken to reveal Hesiod's interest in the nature of both divine and human knowledge. Homer's and Hesiod's contributions to an archaic epistemology serve as evidence that the mythical worldview was not as irrational as once assumed. Karl Popper writes of the need in modern philosophy to return to the "simple and straightforward *rationality*" of the

---

[26] Unless otherwise indicated, all citations from Hesiod are drawn from *Hesiod, The Homeric Hymns, Epic Cycle, Homerica*, trans. Hugh G. Evelyn-White (Cambridge, MA: Harvard University Press, 1914).

[27] Snell, 139.

[28] See Snell, 138-39. Also, see W. J. Verdenius, "Notes on the Proem of Hesiod's *Theogony*," *Mnemosyne* IV, 25 (1972): 225-60.

[29] See Verene, *Philosophy and the Return to Self*-Knowledge, 200. See also Ann Bergren, "Language and the Female in Early Greek Thought" in *Weaving Truth: Essays on Language and the Female in Greek Thought* (Washington, D.C.: The Center for Hellenic Studies, 2008), 13-42.

Presocratics, which was apparent in their cosmological inquiries, but particularly in their epistemological concerns. He claims: "There is at least one philosophical problem in which all thinking men are interested: the problem of understanding the world in which we live, including ourselves, who are part of that world, and our knowledge of it."[30]

This could also accurately describe the project that the archaic poets themselves undertook. Although they carried out this task using substantially different means than those of the Presocratics, the poetic tradition provided an important framework for these later thinkers. When these first philosophers began to explore and articulate cosmological questions about the nature of the world or epistemological questions regarding the limits of human knowledge, they could draw upon a set of shared assumptions about the sources and methods appropriate to these inquiries as well as a set of its acknowledged paragons, Homer and Hesiod.

The Three Senses of a Presocratic "Poetics"

By not attributing a blanket irrationality to the mythical worldview, we can acknowledge and appreciate the ways in which it possessed a sort of latent rationality, which the Presocratics succeeded in bringing to the surface and transforming into philosophy. This shift from *muthos* to *logos* was tenuous at times and not without occasional regression in both form and content. It was not at all unusual that the early Greek thinkers would exhibit a certain dependence a upon the basic poetic "texts" of their culture and that these works would provide the background against which they would develop their own theories. This dependence was coupled with the philosophical urge to overcome the dominance and the perceived deficiencies of the poetic tradition. These two tendencies resulted in an ambivalent attitude on the part of the Presocratics toward the works and wisdom of the archaic poets, and from this ambivalence allegory originated as an attempt to resolve it.

In his essay, "The poetics of early Greek philosophy," Glenn W. Most provides a framework in which we can consider the practice of allegory among the Presocratics.[31] He outlines three senses in which the

---

[30] Karl Popper, "Back to the Pre-Socratics: The Presidential Address," *Proceedings of the Aristotelian Society* 59 (1958-59), 1.

[31] The following is, in part, a condensed and selective synopsis of Glenn Most's "The poetics of early Greek philosophy" in *The Cambridge Companion to Early Greek Philosophy*, ed. A. A. Long (Cambridge: Cambridge University Press, 1999), 332-62.

early Greek thinkers employed and were influenced by what we now refer to as the discipline of "poetics."

1. Poetics as explicit. The first sense that Most distinguishes is the *explicit* or conscious form of poetics that was included as part of the Presocratics' manifold investigations into physical and metaphysical reality. The Presocratics reflected about poetry, just as they reflected about nature and knowledge. In this sense, according to Most, they had a poetics in much the same way that they had a cosmology or epistemology. The notion of an explicit poetics is relevant to the present discussion for two reasons. First, it traces the ancient quarrel between philosophy and poetry back to the Presocratics, rather than to Plato, who is traditionally considered as having initiated the dispute in Book X of the *Republic*.[32] Xenophanes and Heraclitus are central figures here and together form the basis of what can be called an explicit poetics among the early Presocratics. Second, it involves the method of allegorical interpretation of the poets, employed by early Greek thinkers such as Theagenes of Rhegium and the author of the Derveni papyrus, in the effort to rescue them from such critiques.

There is good reason to situate the first articulation of the quarrel with the poets among the Presocratics. Most asserts that, while their views about poetry range from admiration and acknowledgment to hostility and rejection, above all, "the early Greek philosophers' explicit poetics often seem to express their distance from the established authorities of Greek poetry" and that "they seem to be carving out for themselves a discursive space that would be autonomous and privileged over other forms of social communication."[33]

Consider the following admissions of Xenophanes and Heraclitus: "Since the beginning all have learnt in accordance with Homer . . ." (fr. 10) and "Hesiod is the teacher of very many . . ." (fr. 57). These acknowledgements are followed, however, by scathing criticisms of the poets and the techniques employed in their education of Greek society. Xenophanes, a poet himself, criticizes Homer and Hesiod because they violate two important aspects of his own philosophy—his moral reservations regarding the nature of the divine and his skepticism

---

I have omitted sections where necessary and elaborated on many of Most's insights in order to draw out their relevance and significance to the present discussion.

[32] See Gerard Naddaf, "Allegory and the Origins of Philosophy," in *Logos and Muthos*, ed. William Wians (Albany, NY: SUNY Press, 2009) 106-108. See also Chapter 3 herein.

[33] Most, 334.

regarding the nature of human knowledge. Heraclitus attacks the poets on the grounds that their teachings—characterized by multiplicity and inconsistency—are an offense to his conception of universal law (*logos*). We have seen how both of these two Presocratics rejected the poetic appeal to external and divine authority as the only source for human knowledge. This distancing from the mythical tradition through critique not only becomes an integral part of a Presocratic explicit poetics, but also serves as a means of philosophical self-realization for these early thinkers.

Popper claims that the secret to the originality and genius of the Presocratics was its dedication to *critical discussion*. All of the Presocratics, with the exception of the Pythagoreans and the Sophists, engaged in a critique of their predecessors theretofore unprecedented. This spirit of critique took place within the various Presocratic schools, even though these schools were not as structured as those formed later under Plato and Aristotle. According to Popper, prior to and even during the Presocratic era, the nature and purpose of schools was to impart a definite doctrine and preserve it, pure and unchanged. However, the Presocratic schools of thought were not dogmatic in this sense. They signaled a radical break with the primitive or mythical tradition insofar as they created a *new* tradition—one that allowed critical discussion between other schools and within the same school. Popper traces the rise of this tradition back to Anaximander's criticism of Thales and to Thales himself, who must have introduced and encouraged the idea of criticism within the Ionian school if his own pupil was to employ it with regard to him. It was this dedication to critique that prompted the Presocratics to engage with their predecessors in the way that they did, and to do so without fear of disrupting the well-established poetic tradition.

Essential to the critical method initiated by the Presocratics was allegorical interpretation, pursued in a double sense. This double sense of allegory allowed them freely to criticize the primitive views espoused by their predecessors, but in a way so as to retain and utilize any of their proto-philosophical insights. This intention can even be detected in Xenophanes's and Heraclitus's rejection of the poets and their spurious methods. Initially, this comes about through a critique of the seemingly irrational and inexplicable state of divine possession (*enthousiasmos*) to which the poets attributed their poetic prowess. We know from certain testimonia that later in the fifth century the pluralist Democritus emphasized this notion of *enthousiasmos* and that Plato eventually took it up in his own poetics as evidence for his view that poets were not able to give an account (in the sense of *logos*) of what they claimed to know through inspiration. That true knowledge could come from such a state was inadmissible for the first philosophers, yet to deny such a claim would be to discredit not only the archaic poets but also the entire structure of literature and education upon which Greek culture was based. Allegorical interpretation thus emerges as a way to reconcile the poet, and the culture at large, with the philosopher.

In fact, the extent to which the allegorist truly differs from the philosophical critic of the poetic tradition is debatable. Consider Most's description of this figure: "Like the enemy of poetry, the allegorist believes that the only true doctrine is the one the philosopher possesses; but instead of simply recognizing that the poet's text, on its most obvious reading, is incompatible with that doctrine, the allegorist goes a step further and claims that, though the poet may seem to be saying one thing that contradicts the truth, in fact he means another thing that is entirely compatible with it."[34] In trying to render the poet compatible with the philosopher, the allegorist appeals to the opposition between appearance (*doxa*) and truth (*aletheia*) and applies it to poetic texts.

This philosophical terminology was common by the fifth century, but the practice of *allegoresis* is thought to have begun almost a century before, with Theagenes of Rhegium. Theagenes (b. 529-52) was the first thinker credited with having written an allegorical exegesis of Homer as a reply to the poet's detractors.[35] It has also been suggested that Pherecydes (fl. sixth century), one of the first writers to communicate philosophical musings in prose, had already allegorized Homer in a positive sense sometime earlier during the sixth century.[36] These two figures are distinguished from the more prominent Presocratic allegorists by the fact that, for them, the process of reading doctrine into the myths of Homer and Hesiod coincides with the process of reshaping these myths for their own purposes. This is also the case with the author of the Derveni papyrus, which dates back to the late fifth century. Here, the unknown author allegorically interprets an Orphic poem in order to demonstrate that its real sense was consistent with the cosmology of Anaxagoras, Diogenes of Apollonia, and other early Greek thinkers.

---

[34] Most, 339-40.

[35] See scholium to Venetus B manuscript, attributed to the Neoplatonist philosopher Porphyry (234-c.305 CE).

[36] See J. Tate, "The Beginnings of Greek Allegory," *The Classical Review* 41, no. 6 (1927): 214-15.

The later sophistic project of interpretation is important in the history of *allegoresis*. Gorgias, Hippias, Prodicus, and Protagoras are most often connected with the development of rhetoric in fifth century Greece. They were primarily concerned, not with the truthfulness of a given literary discourse, but rather with its effect on the audience. Most considers these figures as relevant to the history of literary criticism rather than to philosophical poetics, but they shed some light on how *allegoresis* served more than one purpose in early Greek thought. Kathryn Morgan clarifies this sense of philosophical poetics by drawing a distinction between the "transformative" attitude toward myth of the earlier Presocratics and the "appropriative" attitude towards myth of the Sophists. With the former attitude, myths were interpreted and composed in accordance with philosophical doctrine. With the latter, the stories were for the most part left unchallenged, but they were manipulated for the sake of exploiting both the status of the poets and the potentially powerful effects of their language on a given audience.[37] While they did not engage in *allegoresis* in a strictly philosophical sense, the Sophists contributed to an explicit poetics and even anticipated a second sense of such interpretation.

2. *Poetics as implicit.* The second sense of a Presocratic poetics that Most distinguishes is termed *implicit* because it refers to those unconscious forms of poetic influence to which the early Greek thinkers were subject. It is important to note that the poetry of Homer and Hesiod not only governed the way in which public discourse was conducted in archaic Greece, it continued to shape the discursive parameters of later Greek culture for many centuries. None of the early philosophers could avoid the direct or indirect influence of these poets on Greek literature, education, and culture. Most claims that as a consequence of this influence, "some of the fundamental criteria that the early Greek philosophers were obliged to try to satisfy in their reflections upon the cosmos and in their communication of these reflections to their listeners and readers inevitably bear a striking affinity to the most prominent features of the works of Homer and Hesiod."[38] This poetics is deemed implicit because any ancient Greek who was producing public discourse in this period could be said to have undergone that same influence. In their intellectual pursuits, the

---

[37] Kathryn A. Morgan, *Myth and Philosophy from the Presocratics to Plato* (Cambridge: Cambridge University Press, 2000), 89.
[38] Most, 334.

Presocratics were not attempting to rival Homer or Hesiod, but they were still subject to their mythical worldview.

In order to understand how the "poetic excellence" of Homer and Hesiod could have turned these figures into the great educators of an entire society, Most examines the five "poetic goals" that they set for themselves and, in large part, attained. The first goal is *truthfulness*. While modern readers might admire the imagination and inventiveness of the archaic poets, for their part, Homer and Hesiod claim that their poetry is valid because it tells the truth. The role that the Muses play for both poets has already been treated in the discussion of their contributions to an archaic epistemology, but it bears some repeating here. The truthfulness of their epics stems directly from the divine knowledge of the omnipresent Muses, who know of things "that are and that shall be and that were aforetime" (*Theog.* 36-37). This ideal of truthfulness is later taken up by the Presocratics as the very essence of philosophical discourse. Xenophanes is the first thinker to delve into the limits of human knowledge, but in doing so, he does not abandon the underlying principle that absolute truth exists, only that man is unable to attain it. Later thinkers, such as Heraclitus, Parmenides, and Empedocles, will all also pursue this goal through both philosophical and poetic means.

The second and third poetic goals are *essentiality* and *comprehensiveness* of content, respectively. Homer and Hesiod both take up the most important subjects as the themes of their works. While Homer's two works epitomize the heroic epic in both its form and content, Hesiod's cosmogonical and theogonical works focus on the origins and development of the universe and the gods. The content of both poets' works expresses essentiality in the largeness of their themes—war as the supreme form of human interaction and displacement (*Iliad* and *Odyssey*), the divine ordering and governing of the universe (*Theogony*), the fundamental conditions of human existence (*Works and Days*), etc. Regarding the third goal, Most argues that Homer and Hesiod, unlike other traditional oral poets of the time, "recognized in the new technology of writing an opportunity for creating works which brought together within a single compass far more material than could ever have been presented continuously in a purely oral format."[39] This allowed them to point beyond

---

[39] Most, 344.

the essential themes in their epics to other parts of cultural knowledge in general.[40]

The Presocratics can be seen to have adopted these poetic goals in their own philosophical pursuits. Beginning with the Ionians, the philosopher's task was not to attain knowledge of just any facts about the natural world, but rather to seek the *arche*, the first and sustaining principle of the cosmos. The goal of essentiality for the first philosophers is also revealed by their positing of a *single* substance as the principle underlying the multiplicity inherent in the world. Later thinkers, such as Xenophanes, extended this singularity to the nature of the divine; the Heraclitean positing of *Logos* as universal law is another example of the interpretation of essentiality in a numerically reductive sense. This reductionism did not prevent them from adopting the poetic goal of *comprehensiveness*. They sought to discover the *one* cause (or, for certain later thinkers, the relatively small number of causes) that would explain *everything else*. Examples of this include Anaximander's *apeiron*, Anaximenes's *aer*, Heraclitus's *Logos*, and Anaxagoras's *Nous*, among others. Ultimately, the Presocratics might be said to have expressed an even greater interdependence than the archaic poets of essentiality and comprehensiveness of content as philosophical goals.

The third poetic goal that can be attributed to the poets is *narrative temporality*. The epic poetry of Homer and Hesiod demonstrate a refinement of the narrative techniques employed by Greek poetry in general. This refinement is perhaps obvious in Homer's works, but as Most points out, even Hesiod adds a narrative dimension to his material. In the *Theogony*, "he does not present his theological system in the form of a static catalogue but instead establishes relations of consanguinity, alliance, and hostility among his gods so that they can both enter into smaller narrative relations with one another and also form part of the larger story."[41] Although it might seem odd to ascribe this particular poetic goal to the Presocratics, there are certain parallels to be drawn. The account of the cosmos given by the early Greek thinkers was not of a static system, but rather of a dynamic world in which things are continually coming into being and passing away. The best example of narrative temporality in the Presocratics is found in Empedocles's cosmic story of love and strife.

---

[40] Cited as examples of this are Homer's insertion of the Catalogue of Ships in the *Iliad* and Hesiod's reference to local divinities acknowledged throughout the Greek world. See Most, 344-45.

[41] Most, 345.

The fourth goal is the poet's preference for *macroscopic form* over microscopic precision. Despite the poetic excellence embodied by Homer and Hesiod, there is a lack of formal organization in their works. In Homer, central themes are sometimes subordinated to secondary episodes; in Hesiod, there are frequent gaps in the progression of thought from one section to the next. The preference for macroscopic form is also evident in the Presocratic project of philosophy. This preference may, in part, be a function of the incomplete nature of the sources on the early Greek thinkers, but it can also be seen in some of the extant fragments and testimonia. Like the archaic poets, many of the first philosophers were not particularly concerned with establishing a rigorously coherent system, but rather devoted their attention to individual formulations. The Ionians are associated with isolated doctrines positing their respective originating principles. Heraclitus's book is considered a collection of aphorisms, and Zeno's work is one of paradoxes and individual arguments. These are but a few of the examples of the ways in which the poetic ideals of *truthfulness, essentiality, comprehensiveness, narrative temporality,* and *macroscopic form* were appropriated by and found expression in the Presocratic project of an implicit poetics.

3. *Poetics as immanent.* The third sense that Most distinguishes is the *immanent* poetic character of much of the work of the early Greek philosophers. Despite the reservations of certain Presocratics about the methods employed by the archaic poets—and the outright rejection of their claims to truthfulness—other early Greek thinkers deliberately chose to express their philosophical positions through poetic means. The most obvious examples of this type of poetics are the works of Xenophanes, Parmenides, and Empedocles, in which views are expressed in verse, in the traditional meter of Greek epic poetry. Other early thinkers, such as Heraclitus, though not writing in verse, nonetheless utilized aphorisms and other types of figurative language in articulating their positions. This was astonishing, given the fact that by the sixth and fifth centuries, prose had become the established medium for philosophical discourse. Even those Presocratics, such the Ionians, who wrote strictly in prose, reveal the frequent tendency to employ poetic similes to illustrate their philosophical principles.

There has long been speculation as to why certain Presocratics employed poetic language while others did not. Most claims that this reflects "the generic difference between prose and poetry with the geographical difference between Ionia in the East and Magna Graecia in the West, opposing what is taken to be the hard-nosed, empirical, innovative attitude of the Ionian tradition with a more conservative, mystical tendency in the West."[42] Others have argued that the early Greek thinkers who chose to write in verse did so in order to cast their insights into forms that would be more impactful and memorable for their audiences.

Neither of these reasons is adequate to explain the Presocratic appropriation of poetry for philosophical ends. According to Most, it is ultimately a matter of linking the choice of poetic language to each thinker's specific situation and aims. In the case of all of these thinkers, it is fair to say that we cannot begin to understand fully their choice of discursive form if we divorce it from their philosophical positions. But the opposite holds true as well—that we cannot understand their philosophical positions if we divorce them from their chosen discursive form. The immanent sense of a Presocratic poetics is perhaps the most significant of the three senses because it suggests the possibility of a philosophical myth, a true reconciliation of poetry and philosophy that first expresses itself through the language of allegory.

Presocratic Allegorical Practices

Having considered the background against which the Presocratic practice of allegory emerges, including the role of the Presocratics in the shift from *muthos* to *logos*, the ways in which they were influenced by archaic poetry and its philosophical anticipations, and the three senses in which one might speak of a Presocratic poetics, we may turn to specific instances of allegorical interpretation and composition among these early Greek thinkers. These compositions occurred in various stages. The first stage involves the subtle reception of the poets once philosophical thought begins to supersede the long-established mythical tradition. This reception occurs with the Ionian thinkers, particularly Anaximander, at the outset of early philosophical speculation.

The second stage is the explicit rejection of the poets because they are seen to violate many of the rational tenets that were already becoming an integral feature of Presocratic thought. The key figures in this regard are Xenophanes and Heraclitus, both of whom object to the poets' role as the main educators of culture and initiate a quarrel with them on intellectual grounds. The third stage introduces *allegoresis* as a way to

---

[42] Most, 351.

save the poets from this quarrel and to appropriate their wisdom for philosophical purposes. This stage includes peripheral figures such as Pherecydes of Syros, Theagenes of Rhegium, and the author of the Derveni papyrus, but also later, more prominent Presocratic thinkers such as Anaxagoras, Metrodorus of Lampsacus, Democritus, and Diogenes of Apollonia. The fourth stage consists in a return to myth with the philosopher-poets, Parmenides and Empedocles, as the central figures. Because this return to myth is mediated by allegory, however, it results in the "philosophical myth," which is later taken up and reshaped by Plato.

These are not necessarily stages in a chronological sense, for there is much overlap in the practices of allegorical interpretation and composition among the Presocratics. Moreover, different thinkers manifested the poetic influence on their thought in different ways. For instance, Anaximander's only extant fragment is allegorical in a direct sense, but other views attributed to him reveal the implicit influence of the mythico-religious mindset on his cosmology. Empedocles, almost a century after Anaximander, also engaged in allegorical composition, though in the form of verse. Since his extant fragments are more extensive than those of any other Presocratic, it is easier to identify the poetic influence on his thought as a whole.

Parmenides also chose the medium of poetry and employed allegory rather extensively in his metaphysical and cosmological poem, *On Nature*, though only a relatively small portion of this work remains. The influence of the poets can even be detected in the writings of Xenophanes and Heraclitus, who were otherwise known to be harsh critics of Homer and Hesiod; they indirectly formulated an explicit poetics in the act of distancing themselves from the mythic tradition. Both exhibit an attempt to break free from myth and its deficiencies, but the language they use in expressing their views reveals the tension that characterizes the shift from *muthos* to *logos* during the Presocratic era.

Thinkers who could be classified as allegorists included both early and late figures within the Presocratic movement. Some merely dabbled in *allegoresis*, while others devoted much of their energy to interpreting the poets in order to either defend or appropriate them. Theagenes and Pherecydes, as mentioned above, had already begun the project of allegorical exegesis long before the fifth century monists or pluralists developed their own interpretation of the poets. There are also the Sophists, who, in contrast to earlier Presocratics, were fundamentally moral and social thinkers.

These later figures, undertook their own allegorical project concerning the poets, but with different aims than those of their predecessors. Their treatment of myth and poetry can be divided into two main areas: as primary texts for analysis, or traditional *allegoresis*, and as the subject matter through which they could display their rhetorical expertise. The latter shows how the Sophists were ultimately more concerned with the appropriation of myth as public display pieces (*epideixeis*) rather than as sources of latent philosophical wisdom.[43] This practice distinguishes them from other Presocratics for whom allegory was, to varying extents, an integral part of their own philosophical positions.

The foregoing supports the view that most of the early Greek thinkers, in some way or another, contributed to a poetics, whether explicit, implicit, or immanent. Behind all three of these senses of a Presocratic poetics lies the problem of language and how adequately it corresponds to reality. Whether and to what extent the project of speculative philosophy can be carried out depends on this problem. One of the main reasons that the Presocratic philosophers found themselves at odds with the mythical tradition was that they believed that the poets, in formulating their account of the whole, had misused language in significant ways. They thus took them to task, by directly or indirectly rejecting both their views *and* their language, and by developing their own poetics, with allegory at its core. This poetics was formulated in a rather subtle and often inconsistent manner, which makes a study of Presocratic allegorical practices both an alluring and a challenging task. Nevertheless, using the above four stages as the framework against which their contributions can be considered, we may begin with the Ionian thinkers and the earliest instances of Greek philosophical allegory.

Of the three figures who make up the Milesian school, Anaximander is the best source of actual allegorical practice. The contributions of Thales and Anaximenes come mainly in the form of their supposed material monism, which stands in direct contrast to the cosmogony of Homer and Hesiod. A fundamental feature of myth is the multiplicity of causes it incorporates into its account of the whole. This multiplicity is apparent in the positing of a hierarchy of gods in its formulation of a cosmogony. While Hesiod traces the origins of the world back to interrelations of Chaos, Gaia, Tartaros, and Eros, Thales posits a single entity, purportedly

---

[43] See Morgan's in-depth discussion of the Sophists and their contemporaries, 89-131.

water, as the *arche* of all things.[44] Anaximenes posits air (*aer*) as his material principle and likens its function to that of the soul: "As our soul being air holds us together and controls us, so does wind and air enclose the whole world" (DK 13B2).[45] Later sources attribute to Anaximenes the view that this *arche* was divine insofar as its nature was infinite and it governed all things. Even in his "simple and unsuperfluous" language, we can detect a new conception of divinity, which replaces the traditional mythological gods but which is not without poetic influence.

Anaximander's extant fragment, quoted earlier in the discussion of the religious concepts that were appropriated by the Presocratics, can now be considered in terms of its allegorical dimension. He writes: "The source from which existing things derive their existence is also that to which they return at their destruction, according to necessity; for they give justice and make reparation to one another for their injustice, according to the arrangement of Time" (fr. 1). Simplicius, the source of this fragment, comments on the "rather poetical terms" that Anaximander employs here. Strictly speaking, he is using an anthropomorphic metaphor, but recall that during this early stage in philosophical thought, the distinctions between allegory and other rhetorical tropes (such as metaphor and personification) are somewhat blurred.

Remarkable is the fact that Anaximander would choose to express his cosmological theory of opposites in poetic language at all. In this single fragment, he expresses his theory of opposites, which explains how things come in and out of being from the *arche* that he posits elsewhere, the indefinite (*apeiron*). It encapsulates the first systematic cosmology set forth by an early Greek thinker—a primary substance, the order or disposition of this substance, and the process by which this order arises. Yet it is couched in moral language, which shows that while he is carrying forward the Presocratic project of narrating the whole in rational terms, he is not at the point of relinquishing the old world view of the poets. Frankfort concludes: "Anaximander presents a curious hybrid of empirical

---

[44] Kirk et al. attribute Thales's views that water is the source of all things and that the earth floats on water to his direct contact with near-eastern mythological cosmology. So, while his views are based on neither the archaic Greek conceptions passed down by Homer and Hesiod nor on mythical formulations to express them, there is still a detectable mythic element to his thought (91-93).

[45] For testimonia of the Presocratics that are not included in Kathleen Freeman's translation of the extant fragments in Diels, I am relying on Kirk's translation of H. Diels' *Die Fragmente der Vorsokratiker*, 5th to 7th eds., with additions by W. Kranz (Berlin: Weidmann, 1934-54).

and mythopoeic thought. But in his recognition that the ground of all determinate existence could not itself be determinate . . . he showed a power of abstraction beyond anything known before his day."[46]

The Ionian thinkers—Thales, Anaximander, and Anaximenes—thus straddle the line between the poetic and philosophical traditions, and in this respect they may be said to consider only inadvertently the problem of how to receive and integrate *muthos* into *logos*. This problem is developed to a much greater extent by Xenophanes and Heraclitus. Xenophanes contributed to the notion of an explicit Presocratic poetics in a number of ways. Unlike his Ionian predecessors, he turned his attention from cosmology to matters of theology and the limits of human knowledge. One of the more important views ascribed to him in the testimonia concerns his attack on the nature of conventional religion propounded by the poets: "Homer and Hesiod have attributed to the gods everything that is a shame and reproach among men, stealing and committing adultery and deceiving each other" (DK B11).

Xenophanes criticizes the poets for not only treating the gods anthropomorphically but also for depicting them as partaking in immoral behaviors. As part of his constructive theology, he posits a single, non-anthropomorphic deity who is a motionless unity, which stands in direct contrast to Homer's and Hesiod's polytheism. In matters of epistemology, Xenophanes also breaks away from the poetic tradition. He reiterates the traditional doctrine of human limitations as far as knowledge is concerned, but he does so within a philosophical context. He implies that these shortcomings are due not to a lack of divine favor or revelation but to a lack of arduous investigation into the nature of things on the part of human beings.

Xenophanes's importance in the allegorical project of the Presocratics comes from his reformulation of the sources of poetic authority; he denies that there is a privileged realm of poetic truth and argues, on both theological and philosophical grounds, against the poetic and conventional portrayals of the gods and the nature of human knowledge. His position is unique because he utilizes the very medium of poetry to express his views. While he dismisses many aspects of the poetic worldview, he does not abandon the possibilities that the mythological framework allows in grasping and narrating the whole. Heraclitus, despite

---

[46] Frankfort et al., 255.

his equally scathing critique of the poets, differs from Xenophanes in this respect.

Heraclitus does not write in verse, yet he is clearly concerned with the validity of poetic language for philosophical speculation. This concern stems from his dedication to the conception of *logos*. One of the most important features of Heraclitus's *logos* is its universality: "Therefore, one must follow (the Universal Law, namely) that which is common (*to all*). But although the Law is universal, the majority live as if they had understanding peculiar to themselves" (fr. 2). The problem of a private understanding of the *logos*—or universal law—is perpetuated by the poets, whom Heraclitus accuses of expounding a spurious multiplicity through their making and telling of myth.

Although Xenophanes and Heraclitus are only tangentially allegorical, they are important in the development of Presocratic allegory because of their contribution to an explicit poetics. As Most points out, both thinkers "seem to have directed their attention to poetry not for its own sake but to criticize authoritative doctrines in order to clear a space for their own."[47] This moment is a crucial one because, in denying the poets' claims to knowledge and granting them at most an irrational sort of inspiration, the early Greek thinkers laid the foundation for what Most calls "the most important recuperative measure designed to protect the poets against such charges, namely allegorical interpretation."[48] This tradition is exemplified during the Presocratic era by the lesser-known thinkers, Pherecydes of Syros, Theagenes of Rhegium, and the author of the Derveni papyrus, as well as the better known figures of Anaxagoras, his disciple Metrodorus of Lampsacus, the atomist Democritus, and the last of the Ionian monists, Diogenes of Apollonia.

Although there is some debate as to the exact origins of allegorical interpretation, or *allegoresis*, the consensus is that it began with one of two figures—Pherecydes of Syros or Theagenes of Rhegium. The former is difficult to classify because his writings, which express his etymological interests, straddle the line between the mythological and the philosophical. He is the first extant prose writer of ancient Greece, and he likely lived during the sixth century, thus slightly antedating Theagenes. Tate argues that the practice of *allegoresis* can be traced back to Pherecydes and his exegeses of Homer, some of which were preserved by later

---

[47] Most, 339.
[48] Ibid.

commentators.[49] He claims that for Pherecydes, "the process of reading doctrine into the myths goes on side by side with the process of remoulding and extending the myths for one's own purposes" and that in this twofold practice lies the origins of allegorical interpretation.[50]

Tate bases this claim on the assumption that, if an early thinker chose to express his doctrines in mythical language, with the intention of it being taken allegorically, then it is likely that this same thinker interpreted the poetic tradition of Homer and Hesiod as though they were conscious allegories as well.[51] This interpretation implies that these poetic texts are allegorical in a strong rather than a weak sense, a distinction used by A. A. Long in his discussion of the Stoic *allegoresis* of Homer: "A text will be allegorical in a *strong* sense if its author composes with the intention of being interpreted allegorically [while] a text will be allegorical in a *weak* sense if, irrespective of what its author intended, it invites interpretation in ways that go beyond its surface or so-called literal meaning."[52] It appears that Pherecydes's cosmogonical speculations, which include both his approach to Homeric texts and his own writings, can be classified as allegorical in the strong sense.

Although less is known about Theagenes, there is an example of the allegorical method that he supposedly applied to Homer's *Iliad*, which is preserved in a scholium attributed to the Neoplatonist Porphyry. Like Pherecydes, Theagenes employed etymology in interpreting poetic texts, but according to Porphyry, his intention was to *defend* Homer rather than to *appropriate* him. This claim of Porphyry raises another important distinction—that between positive and negative allegory. Positive allegory is a way of claiming the poets' authority for the allegorist's own doctrines; it seeks to appropriate the wisdom of the poetic tradition into the speculative project of grasping and narrating the whole in philosophical terms. Gerard Naddaf explains that the earliest practice of allegory manifests this intention: "Because [the earliest philosophers] were nurtured with the

---

[49] For a detailed treatment of Pherecydes of Syros as one of the forerunners of philosophical cosmogony, see Kirk et al., 50-71.

[50] Tate (1927), 215.

[51] See also Peter Struck, *The Birth of the Symbol: Ancient Readers at the Limits of the Texts* (Princeton: Princeton University Press, 2004) 26-27. Struck agrees with Tate in locating the origins of allegory with Pherecydes. He writes: "What we can say, without speculation, is that Pherecydes had an interest in Homer's poem as a *source of wisdom* about the fundamental structure of the cosmos" (27, italics mine).

[52] A. A. Long, "Stoic Readings of Homer," in *Stoic Studies*, ed. A. A. Long (Cambridge: Cambridge University Press, 1996), 60.

notion that the poets were divinely inspired, as speculative thought developed, so did the conviction that the poets had expressed profound truths that were difficult to define in 'scientific language.'"[53]

This difficulty is precisely what gave rise to allegory as an originally positive exegetical endeavor; it also explains why some of the early Greek philosophers wrote in verse as opposed to prose, since only the philosophers could begin adequately to capture the wisdom of the poets. Negative allegory, however, seeks primarily to defend the original text against potential misreading, but not necessarily with the intention of appropriating any doctrine therein. Morgan argues in favor of this sense of early allegorical practice. She claims that philosophy, before employing myth in any sense, would first have to reject it, since "otherwise a philosophical account of the world could not have set itself up as an alternative but would only have competed with myth *inside* the framework of mythical discourse."[54]

The distinction between positive (or appropriative) and negative (or defensive) allegory is relevant, not only because of its historical value in identifying the motives behind early allegorical practice, but also because it highlights the ever-complex dynamic between philosophy and myth. *Allegoresis* that is carried out with the sole intention of defending the poets is not without its merit, but it tends to fall more in the category of literary criticism. The task of interpreting the poets in order to decipher what can be extracted from the *muthos* and incorporated into the *logos* is of greater significance because it reveals the dialectical nature of philosophy's relationship to myth and poetry. Philosophy struggles to recover what is lost in myth once it is overcome by rational speculation. It cannot unequivocally reject myth because doing so would be tantamount to rejecting its own origins. It thus retains, or at least attempts to retain, certain mythical elements in its account by extracting what it conceives as wisdom from the poetic tradition. The primary way that the early Greek thinkers accomplished this retention of myth was through (positive) allegorical interpretation of Homer and Hesiod, as well as through their own allegorical compositions.

All of the remaining figures in this third stage of Presocratic allegorical practice engage in *allegoresis*, not only in the strong sense, but in the positive sense. Both the pluralist Anaxagoras and his disciple,

---

[53] Naddaf, 110.
[54] Ibid. See also Morgan, 62-67.

Metrodorus of Lampsacus, are described by later commentators as having discovered moral and scientific truths in Homer's poetry through allegorical interpretation.[55] Some consider Metrodorus to be "extreme" in his allegorical orientation because he interpreted the gods and heroes of the *Iliad* as personifications of parts of the universe and of the human body. This interpretation likely reflects the views of his master, Anaxagoras, regarding the relationship of macrocosm to microcosm—both ordered by the governing principle, *Nous*—but also quite possibly reflects his own theories about the nature of the physical world. The author of the Derveni papyrus offers a systematic allegorical interpretation in the form of a commentary on an Orphic poem. Although the author is unknown, there is much evidence that points to the fact that he was a follower of the pluralist tradition; more importantly, it is likely that he believed that "Orpheus (as Homer) was an allegorist who had access to truths about the universe that he covered in enigmas" and that "Orphic theogony and pre-Socratic philosophy . . . are saying the *same* thing."[56]

Democritus, another fifth-century pluralist, is said to have practiced psychological, as opposed to moral, allegory in his interpretation of Homer. He was a believer in poetic inspiration (*enthousiasmos*), which would lead him to accept that Homer was a privileged seer who practiced allegory in the strong sense.[57] Finally, even Diogenes of Apollonia, who is considered the last of the *physikoi*, or those who concentrated on the natural world, considers Homer a visionary figure who spoke truthfully, albeit allegorically, about the nature of the cosmos: "Diogenes praises Homer as not mythically but truly speaking about the divine. For he says Homer thinks Zeus is air, since he says Zeus knows everything."[58]

---

[55] Anaxagoras apparently demonstrated that Homer's poetry was about virtue and justice and thus had moral import for the later philosophical tradition. Metrodorus went on to develop this same principle, but applied it to the poet's treatment of physical questions.

[56] Naddaf, 117. For more detailed studies on the allegorical nature of the Derveni papyrus, see: Dirk Obbink, "Allegory and Exegesis in the Derveni Papyrus: The Origin of Greek Exegesis," in *Metaphor, Allegory & The Classical Tradition*, ed. G. R. Boys-Stones (Oxford: Oxford University Press, 2003); Gábor Betegh, *The Derveni Papyrus: Cosmology, Theology and Interpretation* (Cambridge: Cambridge University Press, 2004); André Laks, "Between Religion and Philosophy: The Function of Allegory in the 'Derveni Papyrus,'" *Phronesis* 42, no. 2 (1997): 121-42; André Laks and Glenn W. Most, eds. *Studies on the Derveni Papyrus* (Oxford: Clarendon Press, 1997).

[57] Naddaf, 116-17; Most, 339.

[58] Philodemus, *On Piety* (6b). From Daniel W. Graham, ed. and trans., *The Texts of Early Greek Philosophy: The Complete Fragments and Select Testimonies of the Major Presocratics* (Cambridge: Cambridge University Press, 2010) 1:443.

It is striking that all of these figures—most of whom were considered pillars of Presocratic rationalism—interpret Homer allegorically in both a strong and positive sense. In doing so, they are implying that there are no new ideas in early Greek speculation. Everything that could be said was already said by Homer and, perhaps to a slightly lesser degree, Hesiod, during the archaic period. This stage thus extends far beyond the senses of an explicit and implicit Presocratic poetics, which are better exemplified by Xenophanes and Heraclitus and early Ionian thinkers such as Anaximander. The deliberately allegorical meaning that these thinkers, from Pherecydes to Diogenes, ascribed to their predecessors anticipates the final stage in the development of allegory during the Presocratic era— the return to myth through allegorical composition. This moment occurs in the thought of Parmenides and his follower, Empedocles, a metaphysical monist and a material pluralist, both of whom could be considered the philosopher-poets of early Greek thought.

Parmenides, despite being the father of deductive logic, not only wrote in Homeric hexameters, but also claimed to be divinely inspired, his "revelation" taking the form of a *muthos* on the metaphysical nature of Being. Furthermore, this *muthos* is delivered by a goddess, who is clearly derivative of the Muses to whom Homer and Hesiod appeal in their own poems, but who differs from them in an important respect. Although she tells Parmenides that he will learn from her "all things" and that her account will be reliable and true, she adds that he himself must assess the arguments that she gives regarding Being. This contrasts with the blind acceptance of the divine authority that is an essential feature of the poetic tradition. It is the demand for critique that provides some philosophical validity to the mythological character of Parmenides's account. Furthermore, the mythical elements of *On Nature* are not to be taken literally, as they would be in the poems of Homer or Hesiod, nor are they intended to serve a merely rhetorical function. What, then, could explain why Parmenides chose to frame his arguments about Being in Homeric hexameters?

Naddaf claims that Parmenides's approach is difficult to categorize because, on the one hand, there is a strong and deliberate sense in which his proem is allegorical; on the other hand, in his references to Homer and Hesiod elsewhere in the poem, he seems to be using the weak and unintentional sense of allegory.[59] This procedure is perhaps because he is

---

[59] Naddaf, 115.

employing allegory in a way radically different from fellow Presocratics, with the possible exceptions of Xenophanes and Empedocles. He couches his deductive arguments in poetic language because something more than literal discourse is required to grasp—and to narrate—the metaphysical attributes of Being.[60] Parmenides has moved from the stage of *allegoresis*, in which the poets are interpreted in either a strong or weak sense, to the stage of the *philosophical myth*, in which original allegories are composed in order to express philosophically what was capable of being captured only in myth.

Empedocles, like Parmenides, wrote in epic hexameters and expressed many of his doctrines regarding natural philosophy and psychology in mythological terms. His four elements of earth, air, fire, and water correspond to the Olympian deities, and his cosmic forces of *Love* and *Strife* are obvious personifications, likely derived from Homer and Hesiod. Empedocles goes further than Parmenides does in his proem and presents himself as a god, who delivers his divine poem to admiring human beings, without the intervention of a goddess or the Muses: "I go about you as an immortal god, no longer a mortal, held in honour by all, as I seem (to them to deserve), crowned with fillets and flowing garlands" (fr. 112). Both Kirk and Most highlight Empedocles's employment of sophisticated poetic techniques—specifically, the repetition of verses and the epic simile—as the means by which he presented and illustrated his doctrines.[61] By repeating verses at specific points in the poem in his discourse on cosmic cycles, Empedocles is not only describing such cycles but also enacting them within the text. He calls the reader's attention to this poetic device when he states: "For what is right can well be uttered even twice" (fr. 25).

Scholars have long considered Empedocles, even more than Parmenides, an inspired philosophical figure, who was closer in both skill and spirit to the archaic poets. Yet this does not detract from the rational character of his philosophical speculations. Like Xenophanes and Parmenides before him, his choice to present his doctrines in allegorical language was not arbitrary; on the contrary, it manifests the sense of an

---

[60] Cf. Morgan's in-depth treatment of Parmenides's poem and its allegorical dimension (67-87). She concludes: "Even when myth fulfills most perfectly its function of expressing truth metaphorically . . . it still, by its very nature confuses being and not-being by expressing what is in terms of what is not. This is, of course, a failing of metaphor in general" (87 n110).

[61] Kirk et al., 283; Most, 356-57.

immanent poetics that the Presocratics consciously developed as they grappled with their unique position as both inheritors of the archaic poetic tradition and inventors of a developing philosophical worldview.

This final moment in the Presocratic contribution to the allegorical tradition may be exemplified only by Parmenides and Empedocles, but it is a significant stage in the development of allegory. In their employment of allegorical language, these thinkers construct an early version of the philosophical myth, which Plato will later develop further and employ in his own philosophy. Morgan offers a succinct description of this type of myth, which grows out of archaic myth, but which also fundamentally differs from it: "Philosophical myth looks in two directions. Its presence in philosophical texts acknowledges what philosophy sees as its irrational past and performs two functions. The enclosure of mythological elements inside philosophical discourse enacts the formal subordination of the world of myth to the world of philosophy. At the same time, it implicitly acknowledges that non-philosophical myth cannot be totally absorbed and excluded if philosophy is to retain coherence as a comprehensible form of discourse."[62]

The fact that philosophical myth originates from the immanent sense of a Presocratic poetics reveals, more clearly than in the explicit or implicit senses of such a poetics, how the early Greek thinkers turned to allegory in an effort to render myth self-conscious. While this also occurs in their application of new criteria of truth and falsity to myths, the act of expressing original doctrines in allegorical language makes the transition from primitive to rational speculation possible for the first philosophers. Although they lacked the terminology to discuss how the interplay of reason and imagination allows this task to be carried out, this question is taken up and answered by Plato, through both his critique and his ingenious use of poetry in the dialogues.

---

[62] Morgan, 41-42.

Chapter 3
Plato on Poetry, Myth, and Allegory

> Imagination is but another name for absolute power
> And clearest insight, amplitude of mind
> And Reason in her most exalted mood.
>
> William Wordsworth, The Prelude

Philosophical Myth in Plato's Dialogues

Although Plato is not as close to the poetic tradition as the Presocratic philosophers, he was keenly aware of the effect that Homer and Hesiod continued to have on the rearing and education (*padeia*) of Greek citizens during the fifth and fourth centuries. Plato's concern with the education of the youth is at the heart of the ethical and political philosophy that he expounds in the *Republic* and other dialogues. An integral part of his pedagogical views includes mythical narratives as part of the educational program for both the philosophically inclined ruling class (*hoi phylakes*) and the many (*hoi polloi*) of the polis. He concludes the *Republic* with the eschatological myth of Er and appeals to mythical imagery several times throughout this dialogue to illustrate his arguments. This use of myth occurs, however, alongside a critique of poetic language and the famous quarrel between philosophy and poetry in Book X of the *Republic*. These apparent inconsistencies in the *Republic* prompt the reader to attempt to determine Plato's real position on the relationship of philosophy to myth and poetry.

Plato's attitude towards poetry, myth, and allegory as modes of philosophical expression appears to be negative. How can the reader overlook the fact that he expels the poets from the ideal state? His scathing critique of poetry is in large part based on its mimetic nature, which appears to be at odds with the methods and aims of dialectic. The very presence of *muthos* in the Platonic dialogues is perplexing, as it is a type of discourse that is generally opposed to *logos*. The account based on *logos* uses rational argumentation to arrive at knowledge (*episteme*) and thus seems better suited to the kind of philosophical inquiry in which Plato engages. The account based on *muthos*, since it vacillates between truth and falsehood, can be expected to produce only opinion (*doxa*), which is inferior, and even potentially dangerous, in his epistemological scheme.

Lastly, Plato criticizes both the means and ends of allegorical interpretation, most explicitly in the *Phaedrus* and the *Republic*, but in other dialogues as well. The practice is ridiculed for its tediousness and is associated with the prosaic thinker rather than with the serious philosopher. It would thus appear to have no real place in Platonic thought.

A closer look reveals that these views do not accurately reflect Plato's attitude towards these literary constructs. Although certain dialogues indeed depict poetry, myth, and allegory in a negative light, other works, and sometimes even the very same ones that are critical of these genres, suggest another possibility. Despite his expulsion of the poets on the grounds that their mimetic art hinders both self-knowledge and knowledge of the Forms, Plato frequently appeals to the authority and wisdom of ancient poets, most often to Homer and Hesiod. The superiority of *logos* to *muthos* does not prevent Plato from employing the inferior mode of discourse of myth, side by side with the dialectic in many of his works. Even the beginning student of the dialogues is familiar with numerous cosmological and eschatological myths constructed by Plato.

Although allegory is deprecated and subordinated to other methods of philosophical inquiry, it also finds its way into Platonic thought. Allegorical composition supplies the imaginative dimension that philosophical discourse, taken by itself, seems to lack. Its counterpart, allegorical interpretation, provides the reader of the Platonic dialogues with a way to decipher otherwise impenetrable epistemological, metaphysical, and ethical concepts. It is quite plausible that Plato employs allegorical language in order to "speak of those things which cannot be dealt with directly," for instance, the Forms of the Good and the Beautiful—in other words, the first principles of his philosophy.[1] These principles are concealed through allegorical composition and subsequently revealed or uncovered through allegorical interpretation.

While poetry appears to be an integral part of Plato's project, it is also important to remember that he chose the dialogue as his main discursive form and advocated, above all else, rigorous and rational argumentation. These two facts suggest that his corpus reflects the aesthetic of the philosophical imaginary, more so than any thinker who preceded or followed him. This aesthetic refers to the imaginative element

---

[1] Robert Scott Stewart, "The Epistemological Function of Platonic Myth," *Philosophy & Rhetoric* 22, no. 4 (1989): 275-76. This point is also made repeatedly by J.A. Stewart in *The Myths of Plato* (New York: MacMillan & Co., 1905).

of myth that philosophy continually strives to recover while still asserting its independence from myth.[2]

The forms that the philosophical myth take in the Platonic corpus are varied. He sometimes employs traditional myths, which he modifies; he also invents myths, although many of these contain elements from various traditions, including archaic Greek and Near Eastern mythology. Plato is at once a myth teller and mythmaker, but these roles do not diminish his role as a philosopher. That he would assume these apparently conflicting roles raises the question of whether philosophical discourse requires on some level its opposite—poetic discourse—as the aesthetic of the philosophical imaginary suggests.[3] Philosophy and poetry can be perceived as two sides of the same coin, though this dynamic would have to be mediated by allegory in order to accommodate both the imaginative dimension of mythical discourse and the rational exigencies of philosophical thought.

The idea that the philosophical imaginary guides Plato's thought is reflected in his definition of the philosopher in the *Symposium*. If Plato is the epitome of the enlightened poet, then Socrates might be called, above all, the quintessential philosopher. Many dialogues depict Socrates in this light. The *Apology* and the *Symposium* are devoted to describing Socrates as the model for the philosophical way of life. In the latter, as each guest at the drinking party gives his encomium of love, the reader notices that the features of the figure of Eros become confused with the figure of Socrates. This confusion culminates in the speeches of Alcibiades and Diotima towards the end of the dialogue.

Pierre Hadot suggests that "the reason they become so closely enmeshed is that Eros and Socrates personify—the one mythically, the other historically—the figure of the philosopher."[4] In lieu of giving his own speech, Socrates relates his conversation with the priestess Diotima, from whom he has learned about the nature of love. Socrates begins by classifying Eros as not a god but a *daimon*—an intermediary spirit between gods and men, immortals and mortals. The story of his birth explains why

---

[2] This concept, employed here and earlier in this work, is drawn from Donald Phillip Verene's discussion of philosophical aesthetics in *Speculative Philosophy*. See also Michèle Le Doeuff, *The Philosophical Imaginary*, trans. Colin Gordon (Stanford, CA: Stanford University Press, 1989).

[3] See Marcel Detienne, *The Creation of Mythology* (Chicago: University Press, 1986) 117-18.

[4] Pierre Hadot, *What is Ancient Philosophy?*, trans. Michael Chase (Cambridge, MA: Harvard University Press, 2002), 41.

Eros occupies this intermediary position. He was born of Poros, the god of plenty, and Penia, the goddess of poverty, and his nature can be explained by this origin: "He is always poor . . . having his mother's nature, always living with Need. But on his father's side he is a schemer after the beautiful and the good . . . resourceful in his pursuit of intelligence, a lover of wisdom (*philosophos*) through all his life" (203d).

The portrait of Eros is the portrait of the philosopher, who is also an intermediary figure, halfway between wisdom (*sophia*) and ignorance. Hadot asserts: "Socrates, or the philosopher, is thus Eros: although deprived of wisdom, beauty, and the good, he desires and loves wisdom, beauty, and the good."[5] While this definition of the philosopher is familiar and straightforward, Hadot goes on to problematize it. The distinction between wisdom and ignorance is a contradictory opposition, and thus admits of no real intermediary. Those who are wise would not love or seek wisdom for the simple fact that they are already wise; those who are ignorant would be unaware that they are not wise, so they would not love or seek wisdom either (204a). The philosopher qua intermediary figure must admit of variation in some sense—he must display, unlike the wise or ignorant man, degrees of wisdom and ignorance. This sense of degrees is possible because of a further distinction within the class of ignorant beings: there are those who are aware of their lack of wisdom and those who are not, the latter being senseless people. The philosopher is the former and in this sense is halfway between wisdom and ignorance. This means that the philosopher will never attain wisdom and become wise, but can, at best, progress toward wisdom.

According to Hadot, this intermediate position renders both philosophy and the philosopher ironic: "[Philosophy] is ironic, in that the true philosopher will always be the person who knows that he does not know. . . . He is not at home in either the world of senseless people or the world of sages; neither wholly in the world of [mortals], nor wholly in the world of the gods."[6] Verene echoes this idea in his comments on irony and its role in speculative philosophy. He identifies the guiding trope of myth as metaphor and irony as the philosophical trope. Irony cannot exist at the level of myth because it presupposes a sense of truth and falsehood, which comes only with philosophical speculation.[7]

---

[5] Ibid., 45.
[6] Ibid., 47.
[7] Verene, *Speculative Philosophy*, 113.

Paul Friedländer links irony with myth, which initially appears to contradict the idea of this trope as peculiar to philosophy. He says: "The myth appears akin to irony, both revealing and concealing; and we may perhaps surmise why Socrates, the ironic man, may—indeed, must— become the inventor of myths, why myths are infused with irony, and why in Plato's ironic dialogues, they find a necessary place wherever a ray of transcendence (*epekeina*) and, gradually, the plenitude of *Ideas* penetrate into this life."[8] Friedländer is referring here not to the myths of the archaic or primitive humanity but to the philosophical myth. He adopts Socrates' definition from the *Republic*—that these stories or *muthoi* are composed of falsehood mixed with truth (377a). In this sense, the myth might rightfully be said both to conceal and to reveal. Since the categories of truth and falsity can be applied to myth only once philosophical consciousness has superseded the mythical, irony remains the trope that characterizes philosophy, its orientation, and its discourse.

The act of concealing and revealing that Friedländer attributes to the philosophical myth is the hallmark of allegorical language. It is the purpose and nature of allegory to be oblique—to create a separation between what a text says (the fiction or falsehood) and what it means (the truth). There are two conflicting demands present in allegorical writing: the need for divergence between the apparent and actual meanings within a text and the correspondence between them. The resulting tension that characterizes allegory is noted by Jon Whitman. He writes: "The more allegory exploits the divergence between corresponding levels of meaning, the less tenable the correspondence becomes. Alternatively, the more it closes ranks and emphasizes the correspondence, the less oblique, and thus the less allegorical, the divergence becomes. In this way, allegory tends to be at odds with itself, tending to undermine itself by the very process that sustains it."[9] This obliquity is inherent not only in allegorical composition but also in allegorical interpretation, or *allegoresis*.

Allegoresis claims to discover the truth or meaning hidden beneath a given text. Once a correspondence is established within the text, between the apparent and real meanings therein, it must be continually sustained through a series of divergences between what is said and what is meant. This ultimately places strain on the text and potentially puts the allegorical

---

[8] Paul Friedländer, *Plato: An Introduction*, vol. 1 of *Plato*, trans. Hans Meyerhoff (New York: Bollingen, 1958), 209.

[9] Jon Whitman, *Allegory: The Dynamics of an Ancient and Medieval Technique* (Cambridge: Harvard University Press, 1999), 2.

interpretation of its concealed meanings on a collision course with itself. Similarly, in allegorical composition, the initial correspondence that is made must subsequently be departed from because the allegorical nature of the text depends upon a continuous divergence between what is said and what is meant.

The oblique nature of allegory highlights the fact that it is always pointing toward a goal that lies beyond it: to express in figurative terms what it finds to be inexpressible in literal terms, or, in the case of interpretation, to decipher and differentiate the real meaning from the apparent meaning of a text. This tension is akin to the one that exists in the aesthetic of the philosophical imaginary. This aesthetic requires that speculative philosophy must capture in language the dynamic of both the imaginary and the rational. This dynamic entails a recovery of the imaginative element of myth, which is impossible to achieve completely once philosophical consciousness has replaced the mythic mindset. While philosophy may come close, it can never fully realize itself because it can never adequately recover its own origins, which lie in myth.

Such is also the fate of the philosopher in regard to his pursuit of wisdom, as Plato expresses in the *Symposium* through both the speech and character of Socrates. The figure of the philosopher, like the *daimon* Eros, is destined to seek always what the philosopher cannot fully possess, and this is why he cannot ever achieve wisdom but be only a *lover* of wisdom. This sense of wisdom is not only ironic but also tragic. Hadot explains: "The bizarre being called the 'philosopher' is tortured and torn by the desire to attain this wisdom which escapes him, yet which he loves."[10] The obliquity of allegory reflects the fate of philosophy and the philosopher on the level of discourse. Since the speculative task involves narrating the whole of reality in language, philosophy must find a way to do this that satisfies both reason and the imagination. It does so through allegory, which can say one thing in speech, but mean something else in thought.

The intellectual bias against myth has manifested itself at various points during the history of philosophy, particularly by those thinkers who view myth solely as a precursor to rational thought and discourse. As Friedländer points out: "Hegel interpreted Plato's myths as representing a necessary stage in the education of the human race, which conceptual knowledge can discard as soon as it has grown up."[11] This view can be

---

[10] Hadot, 47.
[11] Friedländer, 1:209.

traced back to some of Plato's ancient commentators, who believed that his fondness for mythology was proof that he was reverting to the old superstitions of the archaic period. Such fondness for mythology would indeed be problematic, as these were the very vestiges of the old poetic tradition that the new philosophical enterprise was trying to shed. The Neoplatonists, in the centuries that followed Plato, tried to rescue him from such charges by insisting that the myths were meant to be taken as allegorical constructions and that there was philosophical significance hidden within them.

Many interpreters of Plato agree that he consciously and deliberately attributed a certain validity to myth. Snell claims that the earliest Greek thinkers "discovered the human intellect—by reading it into myths."[12] If this could be said of Plato's predecessors, it is plausible that Plato intended to carry out this project, in a more sophisticated way and to a greater extent. Ludwig Edelstein suggests that Plato was well aware of the limitations of human reason. Regarding the problems of the soul and its fate in the afterlife, the metaphysical nature of reality, and the origins of the cosmos, reason can grasp and narrate them only with the aid of the imagination. The myth, which transports the reader from the natural to the transcendent realm, thus becomes a necessary counterpart to rational argumentation. Edelstein goes on to assert that, even "Kantians see in the Platonic myth an instrument by which transcendental feeling is roused and regulated."[13]

The Romantic thinkers of the eighteenth and nineteenth centuries went further, mainly because of the ascendency that the symbol enjoys over allegory during this period. They held that these myths were *symbolic narratives*—expressions of absolute reality, which therefore possessed the validity of absolute truth.[14] Modern scholars, particularly those who were

---

[12] Snell, 206.

[13] Ludwig Edelstein, "The Function of the Myth in Plato's Philosophy," *Journal of the History of Ideas* 10, no. 4 (1949): 464. Edelstein is clearly referring to the school of thought represented in part by J. A. Stewart, who devotes a substantial portion of his introduction to *The Myths of Plato* to the idea that the Platonic myths effect in the reader what he calls "transcendental feeling" or value-feelings. See below for more on this point.

[13] Edelstein also notes the Romantic attitude toward Platonic myth: "According to them, Plato was not only conscious of the limits of rational thought, he also knew that in mythical fantasy, in inspiration which the philosopher shares with the poet, man experiences the revelation of a higher truth, of the suprarational or the divine" (464).

[14] Ibid.

influenced by the twentieth-century French structuralist approach to Greek mythology, did not go as far as the Romantics in their estimation of the nature of Plato's myths, but they still acknowledged that the mythical dimension of his thought was inseparable from its rational dimension.

As divergent as the interpretations of the philosophical myth in Plato's corpus are, they all ultimately point to one fact, according to Edelstein: "the question of the significance of the Platonic myth is linked up with the problem of the relationship between reason and imagination, between philosophy and poetry."[15] The dialectical nature of philosophical aesthetics, in which the imaginary must be coupled with the rational, results in an ambivalent relationship between poetry and philosophy and their resulting types of discourse, the *muthos* and the *logos*. The "ancient quarrel between philosophy and poetry" takes on a greater significance in Plato than it did with such Presocratics as Xenophanes and Heraclitus. Although these earlier Greek thinkers might have initiated the quarrel through their critique of Homer and Hesiod, Plato not only continues this critique but also justifies the inferiority of poetry in regard to philosophy by means of rational argumentation.

It is not surprising that most commentators turn their attention immediately to the quarrel in attempting to decipher Plato's views on poetry. In order to understand the true nature of the quarrel as well as how it may ultimately be resolved, it is important to consider poetry and philosophy in terms of the ancient notions of *poiesis* and *mimesis*. The ideal kind of philosophical speculation can be understood as a particular sort of *poiesis*, one that overcomes the perceived defects of mimetic poetry. Philosophical speculation does this with the aid of the imagination and memory, both of which play important roles in the task of grasping and narrating the whole. The interplay of reason, the imagination, and memory not only offers a potential resolution to the ancient quarrel with the poets, but also indicates a sense in which the positive import of Plato's philosophical poetry can be further explored and appreciated.

The Ancient Quarrel with the Poets

The definition of philosophy (*philosophia*) as "love of wisdom" (*philein* + *sophia*) is meaningful only if the nature of the "wisdom" is properly grasped. In *On Duties*, Cicero defines wisdom as "the knowledge of things

---

[15] Ibid.

divine and human" and calls it the highest of the virtues.[16] In the *Tusculan Disputations*, he repeats this claim and elaborates on it: "Wisdom is the knowledge of things divine and human and acquaintance with the cause of each of them, with the result that wisdom copies what is divine, whilst it regards all human concerns as lower than virtue."[17] Implicit in Cicero's definition is that wisdom simultaneously separates and connects the human and divine realms, the former being but an imperfect reflection of the latter. The implication is that the role of human wisdom is to bridge the gap that separates these two worlds. The principal way by which it accomplishes this is through imitation (*mimesis*).

That wisdom consists in knowledge of both the human and the divine first emerges during the classical period, but it is reformulated throughout the history of philosophy. In late antiquity, Augustine employs this distinction in contrasting the temporal city of man to the divine city of God. In medieval thought, Aquinas uses it to elucidate human law in contrast to divine or natural law.

In the Renaissance "Fable About Man" of Juan Luis Vives, these two senses of wisdom find a most eloquent expression. Vives portrays man as both a fable (*fabula*) and a play (*ludus*).[18] Man realizes his humanity by imitating both the natural and divine realms. This act allows man to attain self-knowledge because in imitating what is other, he ultimately comes to know himself.[19] The closer the human realm comes in its imitation of what transcends it, i.e., the divine, the more perfect it becomes. While only the divine realm can be called perfect in an absolute or unqualified sense, the perfectibility of human nature through the love and pursuit of wisdom suggests the complementarity of these two worlds. The divine injunction to "know thyself" not only brings human beings closer to the gods, but also is the very condition for the good life.

The role that imitation plays in human life is treated by Aristotle in the *Poetics*. Early in his discussion of the sources of poetry, he claims that

---

[16] Cicero, *On Duties*, trans. Walter Miller (Cambridge, MA: Harvard University Press, 1997), I.43.153.

[17] Cicero, *Tusculan Disputations*, trans. J. E. King (Cambridge, MA: Harvard University Press, 1966), IV.26.57.

[18] Juan Luis Vives, "Fable About Man," trans. Nancy Lenkeith, in *The Renaissance Philosophy of Man*, ed., Ernst Cassirer, Paul Oskar Kristeller, and John Herman Randall Jr. (Chicago: Chicago University Press, 1956).

[19] See Verene, *Speculative Philosophy*. He writes: "Self-knowledge in its ancient sense involves a knowledge of what the self is and what it is not, a knowledge of the natural and of the divine as related to the civil and the human" (52).

man is an instinctive mimetic: "It is clear that the general origin of poetry was due to two causes, each of them part of human nature. Imitation is natural to man from childhood, one of his advantages over the lower animals being this, that he is the most imitative creature in the world, and learns at first by imitation" (1448b). In addition to his rational and political nature, then, it is man's propensity for imitation that distinguishes him from all other creatures. In addition to learning by imitation, man is said to take pleasure in works of imitation. Aristotle points out that the pleasure derived from imitation is closely linked with the learning that it occasions, not from its gratification of the lower parts of the soul. For this reason, imitation is especially appealing to the philosopher as lover of knowledge.

Later in the *Poetics*, Aristotle elaborates on the poet as an imitator: The poet's function "is to describe, not the thing that has happened, but a kind of thing that might happen, i.e. what is possible as being probable or necessary" (1451a). Poetry differs from history by describing what might be rather than what has been. Poetry is aligned with philosophy insofar as both types of discourse seek out the universal rather than the particular nature of experiences, the latter being the domain of history. This claim also recalls the universal nature of the speculative task with which both myth and philosophy occupy themselves. Primitive man and modern man alike seek to comprehend and narrate the *whole* of reality, although the accounts their approaches yield—the *muthos* and the *logos*—differ in terms of their form and content.

The mythmaker or poet takes the sensible world as the starting point of his speculation and tries to elevate it to the level of the whole through imitation; the philosopher begins with what transcends experience and seeks to capture and express it in concrete language, again through the act of imitation. Verene describes this phenomenon: "Speculative philosophy is the mimetic impulse of the poets, transformed from imitating the objects of the senses to imitating the whole. Like the poet, the philosopher is a maker in words. . . . The philosopher strives to bring the absolute into words. . . . Words are to imitate the thing, not to represent it but to represent its reality in the word, the complete speech."[20]

Aristotle's treatment of the mimetic nature of poetry in the *Poetics* contrasts with Plato's quarrel between philosophy and poetry in the *Republic*. Although Book X is usually cited as the locus for this quarrel, the critique of poetry begins much earlier in the dialogue, in Books II and

---

[20] Verene, *Philosophy and the Return to Self-Knowledge*, 226.

III. The background against which the quarrel occurs is Socrates's inquiry into which program of education should be established in the ideal state. It is asserted that the soul requires an education in music and poetry, before physical training for the body. Moreover, as this includes the telling of stories (*muthoi*) that are both true and false, it must be coupled with a strict censorship over the storytellers (*muthopoioi*).

Of central concern to Plato is the tendency of the poets to tell false stories about the gods: "Indeed, if we want the guardians of our city to think that it's shameful to be easily provoked into hating one another, we mustn't allow *any* stories about gods warring, fighting, or plotting against one another, for they aren't true" (378b). Book II focuses on the problematic *content* of the myths, that they contain damaging lies about the gods, with both Homer and Hesiod singled out as poets who must be censored. The critique here is reminiscent of Xenophanes's and Heraclitus's rejection of the poets on the grounds that they depict the gods in an unfavorable light. Book III focuses on the problematic *form* of poetry, which further sets the stage for the formulation of the quarrel in Book X.

In Book III, Plato describes poetry's function as imitative in nature. Poetry without imitation is merely narration. The problem raised here is that the poet, as imitator of many things, cannot be the master of any one. This same rule governs the construction of the ideal state itself, in which the guardians, auxiliaries, and producers must each play their own specific roles if the state is to be a healthy one. Socrates argues: "Our guardians must be kept away from all other crafts so as to be the craftsmen of the city's freedom, and be exclusively that, and do nothing at all except what contributes to it, they must neither do nor imitate anything else" (395b-c). He concludes that the only acceptable form of imitation, particularly for the children being reared as future guardians of the state, is imitation of one single thing—the good.

The tendency of poetry to imitate the multifarious is at odds with the proper functioning of the state. On the level of the individual, the desire to imitate many things leads to the fragmentation of the human soul and its faculties. Given that both the content and the form of poetry are deficient, Plato has no choice but to ban this form of discourse. His critique in Book III ends with the expulsion of the poets from the ideal state: "If a man, who through clever training can become anything and imitate anything, should arrive in our city, wanting to give a performance of his poems, we should bow down before him as someone holy, wonderful, and pleasing, but we should tell him that there is no one like him in our city and that it isn't lawful for there to be. We should pour myrrh on his head, crown him with wreaths, and send him away to another city" (397e-398a).

In Book X, the critique of the poets and their imitative art develops into a full-fledged quarrel. It becomes clear that Plato's metaphysical and epistemological commitments preclude him from attributing to poetry the universal character that it subsequently has in Aristotle's account. These commitments stem, in large part, from Plato's conception of *poiesis*. The ancient Greek word *poiesis* covered a much wider range of meaning than the modern word *poetry* that is derived from it. In addition to denoting a poetic composition, *poiesis* can mean any making or creation. There are a number of different ways in which things can be made or created. Plato, in his critique of poetry in the *Republic*, however, focuses on what he considers the least desirable mode of making, *mimesis* or imitation. Not only is the mimetic function of poetry the least desirable from a metaphysical and epistemological perspective, it is also the most dangerous, from an ethical standpoint. Plato views mimetic poetry as deficient insofar as it distances human beings from both the reality and knowledge of the Forms, which constitute the highest degree of being. Worse still, it is potentially dangerous, because in nourishing and strengthening the lower parts of their souls, it weakens the rational part and makes human beings more susceptible to vice.

Plato's use of the term *poiein* refers primarily to the making of poetry in Book X. In keeping with his metaphysical views, Plato considers mimetic poetry problematic because its products are thrice removed from reality. The mimetic artist neither makes the Form, which is reserved for the god alone, nor does he make the particular, as this is the work of the craftsman. His creation is relegated to a copy of the craftsman's work, which is itself a copy of the Form. The mimetic artist makes a copy of a copy. Socrates illustrates this point to Adeimantus, using the example of a bed and the three senses in which it is made: the first is the Form of the bed, which the god alone is responsible for making; the second is the product of the carpenter and his skill (*techne*); and the third is the one the painter makes, or rather imitates (597b). Since the painter, or imitator, copies what the carpenter, and not the god, makes, his product is third from the Form. Socrates concludes: "Then imitation is far removed from the truth, for it touches only a small part of each thing and a part that is itself only an image. And that, it seems, is why it can produce everything" (598b).

This metaphysical defect is coupled with an epistemological weakness that mimetic poetry possesses. Socrates considers the question of whether the imitator is entitled to make any claims to knowledge. He distinguishes between the user, the maker, and the imitator of a thing. A user has the most experience of the thing and can be said to know it; a maker, through associating with and having to listen to the user, may be said to have right opinion about the thing. The imitator can claim neither knowledge (*episteme*) nor right opinion (*orthe doxa*) with regards to the being of a thing because the imitator neither uses nor makes the thing in question. Socrates applies this principle to the poet as imitator: "It seems, then, that we're fairly well agreed that an imitator has no worthwhile knowledge of the things he imitates, that imitation is a kind of game and not something to be taken seriously, and that all the tragic poets . . . are as imitative as they could possibly be" (602b). As argued earlier in Book III, because the poet is an imitator of many things, he cannot be the master of any one. The multifarious nature of the poet's imitations causes him to be ignorant of not only the nature of reality as a whole, but also of the nature of his own creations. He is limited to mere opinions—sometimes true, sometimes false—regarding the things he imitates.

Mimesis is problematic from the standpoint of both Platonic metaphysics and epistemology. Regarding their metaphysical status, the products of the imitator are thrice removed from the reality of the Forms. They are inferior even to the product of the craftsman, who attempts to reproduce, albeit as an imperfect particular, the perfect Form of a thing. The imitative function of *poiesis* is not even capable of reproducing the craftsman's particular. This type of making can reproduce only the appearance of a particular thing as seen from one angle. Regarding their epistemological status, the main objection to the imitator derives from his utter lack of knowledge in creating these reproductions.

Plato does not deny that such depictions can appear realistic; on the contrary, he claims that good painters and poets are capable of making their audience believe that their imitations are real. However, it is this deliberately deceptive aspect of *mimesis* to which he objects most strongly. Plato insists that the well-being of the state and its citizens depends on the character and education of its guardians. This education cannot be jeopardized by the potentially deceptive nature of the mimetic poet. In this way, the metaphysical and epistemological shortcomings of mimetic poetry both become the basis for the more important ethical objection that Plato voices against it in Book X.

The greatest danger of mimetic poetry lies in the threat it poses to the constitution of the ideal state and to its citizens. The poet has the potential to corrupt even decent people, and threaten the city, because he "arouses, nourishes, and strengthens [the inferior] part of the soul and so destroys the rational one, in just the way that someone destroys the better sort of citizens when he strengthens the vicious ones and surrenders the city to them" (605b). This objection is reminiscent of the one that Plato makes against the "counterfeit arts of the soul" in the *Gorgias*.

These arts, which consist of rhetoric and sophistry for the soul and cosmetics and cooking for the body, deliberately deceive us into believing that they promote the health of the body and the soul, when, in reality, their activities consist in nothing more than pandering to emotions and desires. They have no rational basis and thus exercise their function in the realm of seeming rather than being. Most dangerously, they aim at pleasure and gratification rather than at the good. Plato sees mimetic poetry as potentially damaging, akin to the counterfeit arts. The ethical objection that he raises against it is twofold: with regard to human life, it corrupts the natural disposition of the soul; with regard to the constitution of the ideal state, it corrupts the acquired education of the guardian or ruling class, from which the philosopher-king is to be selected.

Plato's quarrel with the poets begins with a metaphysical and epistemological critique of mimetic poetry, but his real objection to it is a moral and a political one. Stanley Rosen advances this view in his discussion of the true nature of the quarrel when he asserts: "the defect of mimetic art is political or moral, not ontological or phenomenological. Its danger lies . . . in the concrete misrepresentation of the moral character of the gods, in a favorable representation of immoral human beings, and in general, in the misuse of mimesis by which the same man is led to imitate many things, rather than the one good thing he imitates best."[21] For all of these reasons—metaphysical, epistemological, and particularly ethical—Plato believes that his earlier expulsion of the poets from the ideal state in Book III is justified. In Book X, however, he says that poetry may be readmitted into the state *if* it can successfully be defended by its admirers: "We'll allow its defenders, who aren't poets themselves but lovers of poetry, to speak in prose on its behalf and to show that it not only gives pleasure but is beneficial both to constitutions and to human life" (607d).

---

21 Stanley Rosen, *The Quarrel Between Philosophy and Poetry* (New York: Routledge, 1988), 9-10.

Imagination, Memory, and Resolution of the Quarrel

Is there a non-mimetic function of poetry that would rescue it from Plato's critique and potentially resolve the quarrel? Rosen observes that there is an ambiguity to the quarrel that stems from limiting the discussion to the mimetic nature of poetry. He characterizes the description of this kind of poetry in the *Republic* as inaccurate and even obtuse. He concludes that Book X, in beginning with the critique but ending with the myth of Er, reveals that the quarrel "is not, and cannot be, resolved. It is sublated into a demiurgic discourse that is neither poetry nor philosophy but philosophical poetry."[22] It is plausible that Plato deliberately restricted his critique in the *Republic* to mimetic poetry for the purpose of highlighting and ultimately rejecting its unsavory character. It would not make sense for him to disallow *all* types of poetry, given his frequent employment of myth and poetic language in the dialogues.

R. G. Collingwood supports this view and suggests that, despite his harsh critique of *mimesis* in Book X, Plato tacitly endorses a non-mimetic form of poetry that would qualify as "good" poetry. Other commentators point out that Plato simply never entertains the idea that the poet might imitate the Forms directly. This would introduce the notion of a philosophical or enlightened poet in the dialogues and would explain, to some degree, Plato's own use of myth. There is also the possibility that the deficiencies of poetry examined in Book X are exaggerated by Plato mainly for pedagogical purposes. Whether and to what degree any of these possibilities is the case, the question remains whether Plato acknowledges an alternative to the mimetic form of poetry that he finds so offensive in the *Republic*.

Are there other modes of making that Plato describes more positively than mimetic poetry? In the *Symposium*, philosophy is presented as the highest form of love because it is the love of wisdom, and wisdom orders all other things. It is also the highest form of *poiesis* since the philosopher, like the poet, is a maker. Both of these figures are makers in words, as opposed to the craftsman or painter, who is a maker of objects or images. Verene elaborates on this point: "The philosopher is an imitator but an imitator of what is, not of what looks like what is. Poetry is a danger to

---

[22] Ibid., 26.

philosophy because both are acts of imitation. They differ in the object imitated."[23]

The philosopher uses the mind's eye in order to imitate the Forms, while the poet uses the bodily eye to imitate particulars in the sensible world. Both begin with the image, but the philosopher strives to move beyond it in an effort to arrive at what is universal. In the *Symposium*, the priestess Diotima describes how the type of maker who finds himself pregnant in soul gives birth to wisdom and the rest of virtue, "which all poets beget, as well as all the craftsmen who are said to be creative" (209a). These makers are distinct from those who, because of their attachment to the corporeal, find themselves pregnant only in body and naively think that it is through physical childbirth that they achieve immortality. The philosopher as maker realizes his immortality through the making of knowledge. Though this knowledge is human in its scope, it possesses an eternal character inasmuch as it copies what is divine.

In the *Phaedrus*, Plato depicts the philosopher, through the figure of Socrates, as a kind of poet. Prior to giving his speech in praise of the lover, Socrates bares his head and vows to undergo a rite of purification as "a follower of the Muses" (243a). Not long after this, he recounts to Phaedrus the myth of the cicadas, in which the Muses are said to reward "those who honor their special kind of music by leading a philosophical life" (259a-d). In Socrates' second speech in the *Phaedrus* on the reincarnation patterns of the soul, however, the philosopher is placed in the first category while the strictly imitative poet is relegated to the sixth category (248d-e). Finally, in the *Laws*, Plato likens the philosophical discourse of the Athenian to a divinely inspired literary composition and even claims that the makers of the state are themselves poets of a sort, since their construction is an imitation of the best and most perfect life, i.e., an imitation of the divine (811c, 817b). All of these passages point to another, loftier dimension of *poiesis* and suggest that there is an alternate form of making that is superior to mimetic poetry. Recalling the aesthetic of the philosophical imaginary, which underlies speculative philosophy— which is itself a kind of *poiesis*, since it is the attempt to "make" reality in language—this form of poetry would have to satisfy both the rational and the imaginative faculties.

The resolution of the quarrel with the poets thus hinges on the existence of another dimension of *poiesis*, an imaginative capacity that

---

[23] Verene, *Speculative Philosophy*, 59.

exceeds its merely imitative function. Plato's view of the imagination is difficult to ascertain because of his subtle treatment of it. It does not appear in any of the early Socratic dialogues, but in the *Republic*, Plato begins to develop a constructive view of the imagination and its epistemological, metaphysical, and, ultimately, poetic functions. In the divided line analogy of Book VI, Plato describes this faculty in light of other mental powers as well as in relation to his theory of knowledge. Imagination (*eikasia*) occupies the lowest point on the divided line. Imagining is a kind of *poiesis* insofar as it is involved in the making of images (*eikones*). Notably, it corresponds to the faculty of understanding (*dianoia*), which is also concerned with images, although only to the extent that they contribute to the acquisition of scientific knowledge.

The close parallel drawn between these two faculties in the divided line suggests that Plato's views of the imagination cannot be restricted to *eikasia*, but should also be considered in terms of *dianoia*. Murray W. Bundy claims: "For each of the two realms of Being and of Becoming Plato has a theory of imagination. There may be an imagination of Ideas, and an imagination of material objects, an activity concerned with knowledge, and a corresponding activity concerned only with opinion."[24] How such a theory may be elaborated depends on clarifying the way in which the imagination imitates things.

In Book VII, Plato appeals to the allegory of the cave to further illustrate some of the details of the divided line analogy. Here, *eikasia* retains its sense as the lower kind of image making, and *dianoia* continues to operate at a higher level of conceptual thought, despite its employment of images. The aim of *eikasia*, or the simple imagination, is to reproduce the particular thing as an image; the aim of *dianoia*, or the understanding, is to use images of particulars only in order to arrive at scientific truth. Socrates had already explained the latter activity to Glaucon in Book VI, using mathematicians as an example: "Although they use visible figures and make claims about them, their thought isn't directed to them but to those other things that they are like. . . . These figures that they make and draw . . . they now in turn use as images, in seeking to see those others themselves that one cannot see except by means of thought" (510d-e). When the faculty of understanding employs images, it is not thinking of them per se, but rather of the Forms that they resemble. The mathematician

---

[24] Murray W. Bundy, "Plato's View of the Imagination," *Studies in Philology* 19, no. 4 (1922): 369.

uses images of the square or diameter only to think about the absolute square or the absolute diameter. This reinforces the superiority of the understanding to the imagination, which employs these images as images and not as a means of arriving at the Forms.

The critique of *mimesis* in Book X argued that the imitative maker is inferior because he deals only with appearances. Since this maker copies the creation of the craftsman, he is essentially concerned with making the image of an image. Images of images would comprise the basest form of image making and thus constitute imagination in its weakest sense. In Book X, Socrates accuses the imitative artist of dealing in "phantasy" as well as in "imagination." Plato's use of two different terms here—*phantasia* and *eikasia*—in reference to the imagination suggests that there are two different dimensions or activities involved in imagining. He uses *phantasma* and *eikon*, respectively, to denote the products of these activities.

The *phantasmata* are mere appearances, the lowest form of images that issue from the imagination. They are particularly dangerous because they foster the subjectivity of the artists who imitate things from a peculiar point of view. The *eikones* are likenesses that also issue from the imagination, but they are superior to the appearances because they more closely resemble the Forms. Bundy describes the significance of this twofold sense of *eikones* for the imitative arts: "'Imagination' leads the artist to deal with the material, the changing, the objects of opinion. 'Phantasy' leads him to an error still more serious: to deal with the individual and the relative. He is by so much farther from the absolute, unchanging ideal."[25]

The imitative artists who are guided by fantasy are the real threats to the ideal state and its citizens. The imitative artist who deals with the particulars may dwell in the realm of opinion, but he has the capacity to use the likenesses he creates to get back to their originals, the Forms. The artist who deals solely with appearances is able and even likely to cultivate the epistemological relativism that Plato was determined to eradicate from the society he was constructing in the *Republic*. While these different dimensions of the imagination had been implied in Plato's critique of the mimetic function of *poiesis* in Book X, their import in offering a solution to the quarrel has been overlooked. The distinction resurfaces in the *Sophist*, perhaps because, in this dialogue, the same charge brought against

---

[25] Ibid., 374.

the poet in the *Republic* is now directed at the Sophist—both have the tendency to corrupt the youth through their use of imitative art.

As part of his attempt to capture the Sophist, the Eleatic stranger divides imitative art into two categories—one that deals with likeness-making and one that deals with appearances (236b-c). In keeping with the terms used previously in the *Republic*, the former may be called "imaginative" while the latter may be called "phantastic." The sophist, like the imitative poet, is accused of practicing the latter and of corrupting the youth with the appearances (*phantasmata*). He professes "another kind of expertise—this time having to do with words" and uses it "to trick young people . . . by putting words in their ears, and by showing them spoken copies of everything, so as to make them believe that the words are true and that the person who's speaking to them is the wisest person there is" (234c). In this context, the art of the sophist is connected not merely with changing opinions, but with false opinion and deceptive speech.

Dividing the imitative art in this way and classifying the sophist as dealing primarily with appearances allows the stranger to differentiate the activities of the poet and sophist from those of the philosopher and statesman. The distinction between *phantasia* and *eikasia*, which was drawn less formally in the *Republic*, suggests that there is an imaginative dimension to *poiesis* that exceeds its merely imitative sense of *poiesis*. This resolves at least some of the defects that plagued it when considered strictly in the sense of *mimesis*. Bundy emphasizes that the imaginative capacity is associated with the higher aspects of imitative art, while the phantastic is associated with the lower aspects.[26] This view is supported by the fact that the noun *eikasia* suggests the verb *eikazo*, which means "to make like," but which can also mean "to get at originals through their copies."[27] This distinction also suggests that the value of a poetic work lies in the degree of resemblance that it achieves, since it is this very aspect of images that awakens or recalls our knowledge of their archetypes, the Forms. Plato's theory of recollection (*anamnesis*) is operating in the background of his views on imitation and imagination.

The import of this sense of imagination can be elicited by appealing to a much later conception of memory and imagination formulated by the eighteenth-century philosopher and rhetorician, Giambattista Vico, in *The*

---

[26] Ibid., 387.
[27] D. W. Hamlyn, "*Eikasia* in Plato's *Republic*," *The Philosophical Quarterly* 8 (1958): 19.

New Science. Vico defines memory as "memory [*memoria*] when it remembers things, imagination [*fantasia*] when it alters or imitates them, and invention [*ingegno*] when it gives them a new turn or puts them into proper arrangement and relationship."²⁸ Vico understands *fantasia* as a primodial power by which human beings first order the world. The power of *fantasia* to bring an object before the mind is distinct from *immaginazione*, which is the sense of imagination as the power to form a given perception as an image, rendering the perception available to be formed as a thought. Imagination in its sense as *fantasia* is productive of the object itself. Imagination or *immaginazione* is a middle term, standing between what is given in perception and what is found in conception.²⁹

In Vico's account, memory is associated with both imagination and imitation. He claims that imagination and memory coincide when the latter "alters or imitates things" (*l'altera e contrafà*). Verene points out that the verb *contraffare* is not to be understood here in the sense of making something false or passively imitating something more real.³⁰ It is an active process, which shapes a thing after the form of the subject. In his account of the origins of thought and language in man's experience of Jove, Vico describes how man first imitated Jove by shaking his body in the way that Jove, or the clap of thunder, shook the sky. Jove is thus remembered through the medium of the body, not as a passive copy but as an active re-creation or active re-presentation of the object in the subject.³¹

In Plato's account, memory also has two senses. The first is similar to what Vico calls *immaginazione*, but the second is what enables the connection between *fantasia* and *anamnesis* to be drawn. The more passive sense of memory is introduced in the *Theaetetus* with the wax metaphor: "Suppose . . . that we have in our souls a block of wax. Whatever is impressed upon the wax we remember and know so long as the images remain in the wax; whatever is obliterated or cannot be impressed, we forget and do not know" (191d-e). The impressions on the wax are no better than the images that Plato criticizes in the *Republic* and elsewhere; they are imperfect and potentially misleading copies of material things,

---

28 Giambattista Vico, *The New Science*, trans. Thomas Goddard Bergin and Max Harold Fisch (Ithaca: Cornell University Press, 1984), 313-14.
29 Donald Phillip Verene, *Knowledge of Things Human and Divine: Vico's New Science and Finnegans Wake* (New Haven, CT: Yale University Press, 2003), 183.
30 Donald Phillip Verene, *Vico's Science of Imagination* (Ithaca: Cornell University Press, 1981), 104.
31 Ibid., 104.

and they must accordingly be viewed as a likely source of error. Although Plato does not explicitly say so, they seem to fall into the category of appearances rather than likenesses.

The second sense of memory in Plato is much more robust. It stems from his doctrine of recollection, by which the soul recovers or recollects within itself the knowledge of the Forms that it possessed prior to its embodiment. The higher form of the imagination—in the sense of *eikasia*—imitates in order to return to the originals, the Forms. It does this through the making of likenesses, as opposed to the lower form of the imagination, which makes only appearances. The close relation between *eikasia* and *dianoia* in the divided line analogy is reinforced by this distinction. The making of likenesses that recall the Forms is akin to the Vichian conception of memory's function, when it puts copies formed by the imagination into a proper order. This ordering, in turn, is akin to the re-collecting that occurs in Platonic *anamnesis*, because it is an active rather than a passive process.

Commentators have suggested that the doctrine of recollection explains the presence of myths in the dialogues. Max Latona argues that *anamnesis* serves as the theoretical basis for Plato's own use of traditional myths, as opposed to the innovations of the poets. The latter, which are essentially arbitrary inventions, do not stand up against Plato's critique of mimetic poetry, inasmuch as they engage in *poiesis* in the lower sense.[32] Regarding the question of whether the myths themselves are subject to simple memory or recollection, Friedländer suggests that they may indeed contain visions of the Forms and thereby be included in the province of *anamnesis*. Plato's own use of the mythical imagery of Mnemosyne, the mother of the Muses, to illustrate his theory of recollection seems to point to some connection between the myths and the Forms being hidden therein, only to be recovered through memory in its active sense.[33]

Plato's conception of memory and its relationship to the imagination may not be as compelling as Vico's notion of *fantasia* as a making-imagination, but it nonetheless provides a potential resolution to the ancient quarrel with the poets. Along with the distinction between the

---

[32] See Max Latona, "The Tale is Not My Own: Myth and Recollection in Plato," *Apeiron* 37, no. 3 (2004): 195-210.

[33] See Jane Harrison, *Themis* (Whitefish, MT: Kessinger Publishing, 2003). She claims: "Plato, in his accustomed way just slightly alters the word, giving us a more strictly accurate term Anamnesis for the mythological Mnemosyne, but with no intention of concealing his borrowing" (513).

higher and lower forms of the imagination, Plato's conception of memory rescues poetry from being considered as a strictly mimetic, and thus inferior, kind of *poiesis*. For both thinkers, the imagination is a primordial faculty for human beings, which makes it possible for them to grasp the truth. In Vico's case, this possibility originates from his *verum-factum* principle, in which the true is the made. For Plato, as mentioned above, it is derived from the idea that to imagine (*eikazo*) not only means "to make like," but also "to get at originals through their copies." Bundy suggests how the philosophers and poets might be reconciled through the role of imagination: "Imagination both in philosophy and poetry, in the science of thought, and in the art of expression, is the connecting link between the real and the ideal, between the realm of ideas and that of material objects."[34]

"Other Speech" in Platonic Thought

The resolution of the quarrel depends on a higher form of *poiesis*, one that overcomes at least some of the metaphysical, epistemological, and ethical deficiencies of *mimesis* in the strict sense. While Plato never directly states it, his appeal to poetic language throughout his dialogues implies that philosophy itself embodies this sense of *poiesis*. The emphasis on the dialectic in his dialogues also suggests that philosophy as *poiesis* must involve not only the imagination, but reason as well. Since reason underpins the speculative task once philosophical consciousness supersedes mythical thought, the imagination must operate in service to it, as an inferior yet necessary component of rational thought. Its function is indispensable to the nature of philosophical speculation. The speculative impulse is inherent in primitive and modern man alike, and the imagination allows both to move from the sensible to the suprasensible world.

For primitive man, imagination alone suffices in both the grasping and narrating of the whole. Reason comes into play for modern man because he is compelled to distinguish the particulars in the sensible realm from their corresponding universals in the suprasensible realm. From a Platonic perspective, this distinction corresponds to the activities of the imagination (*eikasia*) and understanding (*dianoia*). The type of account that issues from speculative inquiry—the philosophico-scientific account, in the case of modern man—would thus include both imaginative elements

---

[34] Bundy, 386.

and rational argument, as reflected in the philosophical myths constructed by Plato. This conjunction of the imaginative and the rational would also mean that the use of poetic discourse is an important and even necessary part of his thought, precisely because it expresses the aesthetic of the philosophical imaginary.

The possibility of good poetry in the Platonic corpus might be called part of his immanent poetics, referring back to how this term was used in regard to the Presocratics. Plato expresses all three senses of a poetics—explicit, implicit, and immanent. Beginning with the last sense, it is obvious that Plato has an immanent poetics insofar as there is a consciously developed poetic character that accompanies much of his thought. This includes everything from the brief employment of various rhetorical devices to the construction of elaborate myths that occupy a central place in the dialogues. In this respect he advances the poetic project of the Presocratic thinkers, some of whom used poetic language or devices, but not nearly to the extent that Plato did. He may also be said to have an implicit poetics, which involves those unconscious forms of poetic influence to which most early Greek thinkers were subject. This influence is seen throughout Plato's writings in his frequent appeal to the archaic poets alongside his harsh critique of them. Whether he thinks of Homer and Hesiod as the purveyors of a wisdom that is compatible with his philosophy, he cannot deny their influence on ancient Greek society and its education.

Plato can be said to express an explicit or conscious poetics. That he would develop a position regarding poetry is not surprising, given that he is the first truly systematic Greek thinker. Unlike Aristotle and others who follow him, he does not always present his views on this topic in a clear and focused way. Indeed, his explicit and immanent poetics tend to overlap insofar as the former is embedded within the latter—first, within the dialogues (a poetic form in themselves) and second, in the form of digressions, critiques, and myths. As it has been shown, even the quarrel with the poets in the *Republic* is not an entirely accurate reflection of his views of poetry and its potential import for and role in philosophical speculation. Nevertheless, deciphering the key points of Plato's explicit poetics is necessary in order to understand his attitude toward various forms of figurative speech—in poetry, myth, and allegory. Poetry, in its most general sense, would include myth and allegory; but there are certain elements that are peculiar to it, which can be treated separately from these other types of literary discourse.

With regard to the role of poetry in Plato's thought, there remains the important topic of the divine inspiration (*enthousiasmos*) that underlies certain kinds of poetry as well as the transcendental feeling that such poetry elicits from the reader. Plato's use of myth is considerably more sophisticated than that of the Presocratics. It is thus a better illustration of how philosophy fulfills its speculative task. Recall that the speculative impulse urges the philosopher not only to narrate the whole, but also to do so in a self-conscious way, one that involves both reason and the imagination. This self-conscious approach is precisely what occurs in the Platonic version of the philosophical myth. Plato's critique of allegory remains to be examined. His low estimation of allegorical interpretation must be revaluated given allegory's higher function of enabling myth to become self-conscious and thus making the speculative task even possible. I wish to suggest that allegory is ultimately important and even necessary to Plato's literary and philosophical projects.

In formulating the quarrel in the *Republic*, Plato denies that the poets have wisdom or good intentions, but elsewhere he declares that they are divinely inspired. This view is articulated in some detail in both the *Phaedrus* and the *Ion*, and he alludes to it in other dialogues. In the *Meno*, he clarifies that these individuals may not lay claim to knowledge (*episteme*): "We should be right to call divine ... all the poets, [on account of them saying many true things when inspired] though they have no knowledge of what they are saying" (99cd). Plato does acknowledge that they can be divinely inspired with right opinion (*orthe doxa*), which is lower in rank than knowledge but still of some value within his epistemological scheme.

In the *Laws* IV, he describes the nature of this inspiration through the words of the Athenian: "When a poet takes his seat on the tripod of the Muse, he cannot control his thoughts. He's like a fountain where the water is allowed to gush forth unchecked. His art is the art of representation, and when he represents men with contrasting characters he is often obliged to contradict himself, and he doesn't know which of the opposing speeches contain the truth" (719c). In both of these passages, however, the divine inspiration that Plato attributes to the poet results in a state that is inferior in significant ways. Either it grants him right opinion, but not knowledge, or it makes him appear out of control and self-contradictory rather than measured in both thought and speech.

This theme is further developed in the *Ion*, which is devoted to the point made in the *Meno* regarding the poet's claim to knowledge versus opinion. Socrates argues: "Because it's not by mastery that they make poems or say many lovely things about their subjects (as you do about Homer)—but because it's by a divine gift—each poet is able to compose beautifully only that for which the Muse has aroused him . . . and each of them is worthless for other types of poetry" (534c). The critique here differs from that of the *Republic* in some important respects. Socrates does not accuse Ion, or even Homer for that matter, of deliberately deceiving or corrupting the youth through their poetry or recitations.[35]

Socrates develops the view that poets and rhapsodes speak not from any kind of knowledge but from inspiration. This claim is problematic because, in lacking knowledge, poets and rhapsodes become mere instruments of the gods. This point is illustrated by the famous magnet analogy, in which the magnets represent the Muses, the iron rings attached to them represent the poets, the set of rings attached to those rings represent the rhapsode's or poet's interpreters, and the final set of rings represent the rhapsode's audience. This image captures Plato's idea that no ring is the source of the next ring's attachment to it, which in turn suggests that neither poet nor rhapsode is responsible for his own inspiration.

Socrates goes further in the *Ion* and claims the human intellect and the ability to make or recite poetry are incompatible: "As long as a human being has his intellect in his possession he will always lack the power to make poetry or sing prophecy" (534b-c). This claim anticipates the much longer discussion of the poet's madness in the *Phaedrus*. Although much of this dialogue is relevant to Plato's aesthetics, there is one particular section devoted to the topic of the divine inspiration of poetry. Having defined love as a type of madness (*mania*), Socrates goes on to elaborate on the nature of madness: "There are two kinds of madness, one produced by human illness, the other by a divinely inspired release from normally accepted behavior" (265a).

Four more divisions are made, which classify madness as prophecy, mysticism, poetry, or love. It is important to note that Plato's depiction of the madness underlying poetry in the *Phaedrus* is separated from the ordinary madness depicted in the *Ion* or the *Laws*. This separation is perhaps because he introduces a new figure in this dialogue—the philosopher-poet. As previously discussed, when Plato ranks the various

---

[35] This is perhaps due to the fact that Ion is not a poet himself, but rather a performer and interpreter, mainly of Homer's poetry.

reincarnation patterns, he places the "follower of the Muses" in the first category with the philosopher and the merely imitative artist in the sixth category. This identification of the philosophy and poetry suggests that, just as there may be a good form of poetry, there may also be a good type of madness or inspiration that the philosopher is capable of experiencing and that would positively bear on his thought and discourse.[36]

The attention given both to the divine nature of inspiration and the madness that accompanies it in these dialogues makes it difficult to determine whether Plato ultimately approves of inspired poetry or condemns it. What makes this question even more complex is the corresponding feeling that such poetry is said to evoke in its reader. J. A. Stewart claims: "The essential charm of all Poetry . . . lies in its power of inducing, satisfying, and regulating what may be called Transcendental Feeling, especially that form of Transcendental Feeling which manifests itself as solemn sense of Timeless Being—of 'That which was, and is, and ever shall be,' overshadowing us with its presence."[37] This description of transcendental feeling appeals to the mythic construct of past, present and future, which is traditionally the domain of the Muses, who were said to transmit knowledge of this timeless being to Homer and Hesiod.

Stewart goes on to explain that through his myths, Plato appeals to the part of the soul that is not rational or logical, but to the part that feels, wills, and acts. This is human nature in its most primordial form. The primary effect of the myths is that they are to be felt, not understood. Rather than claiming that this diminishes the import of the Platonic myth, Stewart says: "Transcendental Feeling, welling up from another 'Part of the Soul', whispers to Understanding and Sense that they are leaving out something. What? Nothing less than the secret plan of the Universe. And what is that secret plan? The other 'Part of the Soul' indeed comprehends it in silence as it is, but can explain it to the Understanding only in the symbolical language of the interpreter, Imagination—in Vision."[38]

This transcendental feeling recalls the sense of wonder or awe that is evoked in both primitive and modern man alike when confronting reality. Stewart may be overstating the case to some degree in his insistence upon

---

[36] See F. M. Cornford, *Principium Sapientiae: The Origins of Greek Philosophical Thought*, 62-87. In his chapter "Seer, Poet, Philosopher," Cornford connects these figures and convincingly argues for "the association of poetic and prophetic inspiration with the intuitive wisdom of the philosopher" (66).

[37] Stewart, 22.

[38] Ibid., 42.

the mystical dimension of the myths, given Plato's rationalist commitments. But his description of the transcendental feeling evoked by this type of poetry does point to the presence and importance of the philosophical imaginary in Plato's speculative project. The view that the imagination plays an essential role in both the construction of the myths and in their reception is not only plausible but likely. This other part of the soul, which Stewart identifies as the vegetative, depends on the imagination (*eikasia*) as the interpreter of the hidden meaning that it intuits in myth. This message is conveyed through images to the understanding (*dianoia*), which would otherwise be unable to grasp it since transcendental feeling is not experienced by the soul's higher faculties.

The problem with Stewart's notion of the transcendental feeling is that it overshadows the rational dimension of Plato's thought. The philosophical myth can rely on both reason and the imagination and still evoke a feeling of wonder in regard to the metaphysical principles that are expressed therein. The Platonic myth may have more than one function. It can be understood as both a *muthos* and a *logos*, as in the eschatological myth that concludes the *Gorgias*: "Give ear then—as they put it—to a very fine account. You'll think that it's a mere tale (*muthos*), I believe, although I think it's an account (*logos*), for what I'm about to say I will say to you as true" (523a). It may also serve as a medicine or drug (*pharmakon*), as it does in the case of the noble lie told in the *Republic*: "If what we said just now is correct, and falsehood, though of no use to the gods, is useful to people as a form of drug, clearly we must allow only [the rulers] to use it, not private citizens" (389b). It can be a likely story, as in the *Timaeus*: "If we can come up with accounts no less likely than any, we ought to be content, keeping in mind that both I, the speaker, and you, the judges, are only human. So we should accept the likely tale on these matters" (29c-d).

In all of these cases, the Platonic myth points to the fact that human beings, as opposed to gods, can never know the truth, at least not in its entirety, so myth-making is an essential part of satisfying the human speculative impulse. As Penelope Murray points out, there is a fundamental difference between the myth-making as employed by primitive versus modern man: "The difference between poetic and philosophical myths is that the philosopher is aware of the approximate status of his myths, whereas the poet is not."[39]

The approximate status of myths is what makes allegory necessary to the Platonic philosophical and literary project. Stewart goes to great lengths in distinguishing myth from allegory in Plato's dialogues. He writes: "This is the criterion of Myth as distinguished from Allegory or Parable: Myth has no moral or other meaning in the minds of those who make it, and of those for whom it is made."[40] While the myth, according to Stewart, evokes transcendental feeling, allegories—particularly those that are transparent or contrived—cease to be interesting for their readers and are ultimately forgotten. He concludes: "Allegory is Dogma in picture-writing; but Myth is not Dogma, and does not convey Dogma."[41]

This deprecation of allegory is expressed in Plato's own writings, although it is directed more at the practice of allegorical interpretation than at allegorical composition. In Book II of the *Republic,* Socrates asserts: "We won't admit stories into our city—whether allegorical or not—about [the misdeeds of the gods]. The young can't distinguish what is allegorical from what isn't, and the opinions they absorb at that age are hard to erase and apt to become unalterable" (378d). Plato is alluding to the tendency of the early allegorists to defend the archaic poets by interpreting their writings in a way that made them inoffensive and palatable. This approach to allegorical interpretation is employed by some of the Presocratics. Plato does not think that such a practice solves the inherent problem regarding the false content of these myths. If mythology is to have a place in the ideal state, it must be radically reformed in such a way that it is rendered compatible with philosophy.

Positive *allegoresis,* then, in which a text is interpreted to show how it implicitly expresses certain philosophical doctrines, would seem to be a better solution to the problem. In the *Phaedrus,* however, Plato dismisses allegory as an amusing pastime, not serious enough for the philosopher to pursue. When Phaedrus asks Socrates whether he believes the legend of

---

[39] Penelope Murray, "What is a *Muthos* for Plato?," in *From Myth to Reason? Studies in the Development of Greek Thought,* ed. Richard Buxton (Oxford: Oxford University Press, 1999), 260.

[40] Stewart, 15. Cf. Jaspers: "The myth [during the Axial Period] became the material of a language which expressed by it something very different from what it had originally signified: it was turned into parable. Myths were remoulded, were understood at a new depth during this transition, which was myth-creating after a new fashion, at the very moment when the myth as a whole was destroyed" (3).

[41] Ibid., 242.

Boreas and Orithuia is true, Socrates responds: "Actually, it would not be out of place for me to reject it, as our intellectuals do. I could then tell a clever story. . . . Now, Phaedrus, such explanations are amusing enough, but they are a job for a man I cannot envy at all" (229d). The "intellectuals" to whom Socrates refers are the allegorists of his day, whom he describes as "clever" rather than insightful. He characterizes them as possessing a sort of "rough ingenuity" that can never be brought to full completion since the need to rationalize one myth leads to the need to rationalize *all* myths (229e). Finally, he claims that he has no time for such activities, given his pursuit of self-knowledge (230a). This view is echoed in the *Protagoras* when he complains: "When a poet is brought up in a discussion, almost everyone has a different opinion about what he means, and they wind up arguing about something they can never finally decide. The best people avoid such discussions and rely on their own powers of speech to entertain themselves and test each other" (347e).

Allegorical interpretation, as these brief comments reveal, is problematic. It undermines a fundamental feature of myth—whether philosophical or non-philosophical—as an instrument of persuasion. After recounting the eschatological myth in the *Phaedo*, Socrates asserts: "No sensible man would insist that these things are as I have described them, but I think it is fitting for a man to risk the belief—for the belief is a noble one—that this, or something like this, is true about our souls" (114d). While he does not advocate taking the myth literally, he seems also to reject the idea of interpreting its content to such a degree that it becomes contrived or artificial. The same critique applies to the etymological method, which is the topic of the *Cratylus*. In that dialogue, etymology is described a charming enough diversion or pastime, but one that should not be taken too seriously, given its lack of reliability.[42] Edelstein concludes from these critiques that it would be incorrect to assume that Plato's own myths are intentional allegories He writes: "[Plato] refused to apply allegorical interpretation to the myths of others; he certainly did not wish to have this 'rustic kind of wisdom' applied to his own mythology."[43]

Despite these views, there is a sense in which *allegoresis* may be rendered compatible with Plato's poetics, which stems from his treatment

---

[42] See Timothy M. S. Baxter, *The Cratylus: Plato's Critique of Naming* (New York: Brill, 1992).
[43] Edelstein, 467.

of the poets as divinely inspired figures. It would be futile to ask the poets—or the rhapsodes—what their verses mean, since they can lay no claim to knowledge, only to right opinion at best. The meaning of a poem must be independent of the poet's intention, since the poet did not devise it himself but was rather inspired by the gods to express it in language. It is subject to interpretation. Tate draws the conclusion: "Plato's account of inspiration and the obscure and mythical style in which it naturally expresses itself is really in favour of the view that some at least of the myths of the poets contain deeper meanings which, quite apart from the knowledge or intention of the poets themselves, may be not only profound but true."[44]

This observation does not necessarily change Plato's view that allegorical interpretation is subject to uncertainty. Part of Plato's critique of allegory was based on the fact that it was so closely associated with the notions of *symbolon*, *hyponoia*, and *aenigma*. The view that the oblique expression of a truth (*symbolon*) must be interpreted in order to grasp its underlying meaning (*hyponoia*) so that its enigma (*aenigma*) can be solved is contrary to the aims and methods of the dialectic. If the allegorist is also subject to some degree of inspiration in interpreting the work of the poets, then this need for inspiration also contributes to the uncertainty inherent in *allegoresis*. The mere fact that Plato attributes divine inspiration to the poets in the first place suggests that he believes that poetic expression exceeds the limits of literal discourse. Poetry requires figurative speech and the interpretation that accompanies it because it attempts to express something divine. Like Plato's own philosophical myths, figurative speech is "both a means of thinking about what is grasped in the transcendental experience and a method of expressing it."[45]

The status of the philosophical myth also suggests that *allegoresis* has a place in Plato's thought. The reader must interpret these myths in order to locate their meaning somewhere between truth and falsehood. The non-philosophical myth is taken as a matter of faith. The Muses are the only ones who can distinguish what is true from what is false in the accounts that they impart to the poets. Both the poet and his audience accept the content of the myth as true, *prima facie*. The reason for this

---

[44] J. Tate, "Plato and Allegorical Interpretation," 149-50.
[45] M. John Gregory, "Myth and Transcendence in Plato," *Thought* 43 (Summer 1968): 284.

acceptance is that, for mythical consciousness, the myth is a direct expression of reality—it *presents* the whole as such.

When philosophical consciousness emerges and begins to replace mythical thought, the truth value of the myths breaks down. The oppositions that coalesce seamlessly in these primitive stories are now distinguished and must be reconciled in order to achieve a rational account of reality. The philosopher soon finds that a perfectly consistent and coherent account is impossible to achieve. He returns to myth to search for something that would enable him to narrate reality in a more successful way. He discovers that it is through allegory that he might do this, precisely because it *represents* the whole and allows him to transcend the literal dimension of myth. Allegory, and specifically the practice of allegorical interpretation, comes to supply what philosophy alone lacks.

There also appears to be a sense in which allegorical composition is compatible with Plato's poetics. This complementary procedure of *allegoresis* is frequently employed throughout the Platonic dialogues, but the line of demarcation between allegory and myth in Plato's writing is often blurred. Even Stewart, who seeks to distinguish allegory from myth and favors the latter over the former for its transcendental qualities, admits that there is some overlap between the two modes. He asserts that genuine myth "sets forth a mystery which the scientific understanding cannot fathom," but that it is this very kind of myth that most easily lends itself to allegorical interpretation.[46] The reason that myth can take thought beyond scientific understanding, according to Stewart, is that myths are often constructed of parts, some of which are allegorical in nature. Appealing to the "cave allegory" in the *Republic*, he writes: "[The cave] certainly is an Allegory, and is offered as such together with its interpretation. But when a great poetic genius like Plato builds an Allegory, the edifice, while serving its immediate purpose as an Allegory, transcends that purpose."[47]

Stewart's position, though it still values myth over allegory, nonetheless suggests a place for allegorical composition in the Platonic dialogues. The poet, or in Plato's case, the philosopher-poet, takes on the speculative task of narrating the whole in language. As previously discussed, this task requires the exercise of both reason and the imagination if it is to be properly carried out. Since the rational exigencies of philosophical thought are ever-present, the philosopher-poet cannot be

---

[46] Stewart, 230.
[47] Ibid., 252.

a myth-maker in the same sense as the archaic poets. In the primitive myth, the truth coincides with its expression. The presentation of reality in the myth is the very apprehension of that reality. This power of *presentation* is *muthos* in its most primordial and unadulterated form.

In the philosophical myth, *logos* lurks in the background and necessitates a different kind of discourse, namely, one that is not only imaginative but also rational. This type of discourse requires mediation. Reality can neither be presented nor apprehended directly because man has become, with the advent of philosophy, an objective interpreter of that reality. The philosopher-poet thus turns to the allegorical technique of saying one thing but meaning something else. This allows the philosopher-poet to resolve the oppositions inherent in reality using *representation*—of the divine by the human, of the supernatural by the natural, of the abstract by the particular, and so on.

Plato's ingenious construction of the philosophical myth and its timeless appeal to the reader makes it tempting to place it in the category of genuine myth, in the very way Stewart describes it—"as a mystery that scientific understanding cannot fathom." But as with the transcendental feeling that genuine myth is said to evoke in the reader, Stewart again overlooks the rational dimension of Plato's thought. This view neglects the playfulness (*paidia*) associated with myth-telling. Plato invokes the idea of play several times in the dialogues to describe the nature of the philosophical myth and how it functions with the dialectic.[48] Janet Smith suggests that Plato's use of this metaphor derives from his conception of philosophy as a serio-playful endeavor: "Myth helps the philosophic search by facilitating playing with ideas; it often provides the possibilities which dialectic tests."[49]

The view I have advanced agrees most closely with that expressed by Brooke Westcott. He distinguishes allegory from myth: "In the allegory the thought is grasped first and by itself, and is then arranged in a particular dress. In the myth, thought and form come into being together; the thought is the vital principle which shapes the form; the form is the sensible image which displays the thought."[50] Westcott considers Plato's myth as genuine myth, but does not discount its uniquely philosophical nature. The

---

[48] See *Statesman* 268d; *Critias* 110a; *Timaeus* 59d.
[49] Janet E. Smith, "Plato's Use of Myth in the Education of Philosophic Man," *Phoenix* 40 (1986): 25-26.
[50] Brooke Foss Westcott, "The Myths of Plato," in *Essays in the History of Religious Thought in the West* (London: Macmillan & Co., 1891), 4.

transcendental feeling that myth evokes, on Stewart's view, gives way to the role that allegory plays in its construction. Westcott concludes: "The Platonic myth is, in short, a possible material *representation* of a speculative doctrine, which is affirmed by instinct, but not capable of being established by a scientific process. The myth is itself the doctrine so far as it is at present capable of apprehension by men."[51]

The philosophical myth, especially in the hands of Plato, shows how allegory renders primitive myth self-conscious and fulfills the speculative task of narrating the whole in a way acceptable to *logos*. Plato expresses, in a more explicitly rational manner, the orientation of the earliest philosophers, the Presocratics, who were the first to grapple with the relationship of philosophy and myth. In conceiving of allegory as philosophy's attempt to make myth self-conscious, I hope to have shed new light on a concept with a very long and complex history. Situating allegory within classical antiquity is both necessary and useful, given this period's proximity and its relationship to the mythical age. My intention has been to situate allegory within the field of already existing scholarship in a way that, while not exhaustive, will contribute to a better understanding of its early historical development and its bearing on both the nature and task of speculative philosophy.

---

[51] Ibid., 6 (italics mine).

Selected Bibliography

Adams, Hazard. *Philosophy of the Literary Symbolic.* Tallahassee, FL: University Presses of Florida, 1983.

Barfield, Raymond. *The Ancient Quarrel between Philosophy and Poetry.* Cambridge: Cambridge University Press, 2011.

Baxter, Timothy M. S. *The Cratylus: Plato's Critique of Naming.* New York: Brill, 1992.

Benjamin, Walter. *The Origin of German Tragic Drama.* Translated by John Osborne. London: Verso, 1998.

Bergren, Ann. "Language and the Female in Early Greek Thought." In *Weaving Truth: Essay on Language and the Female in Greek Thought,* 13-42. Washington, D.C.: The Center for Hellenic Studies, 2008.

Betegh, Gábor. *The Derveni Papyrus: Cosmology, Theology and Interpretation.* Cambridge: Cambridge University Press, 2004.

Boys-Stone, G. R., editor. *Metaphor, Allegory, and the Classical Tradition.* Oxford: Oxford University Press, 2003.

Brisson, Luc. *Plato the Myth Maker.* Translated by Gerard Naddaf. Chicago: University of Chicago Press, 1998.

———. *How Philosophers Saved Myths: Allegorical Interpretation and Classical Mythology.* Translated by Catherine Tihanyi. Chicago: Chicago University Press, 2004.

———, Brigitte Pérez-Jean, and Patricia Eichel-Lojkine, editors. *L'allégorie de l'antiquité à la renaissance.* Paris: Champion, 2004.

Buffière, Félix. *Les mythes d'Homère et la pensée grecque.* Paris: Les Belles Lettres, 1956.

Bundy, Murray W. "Plato's View of the Imagination." *Studies in Philology* 19, no. 4 (1922): 362-403.

Burnet, John. *Early Greek Philosophy.* New York: Meridian Books, 1969.

Buxton, Richard, editor. *From Myth to Reason? Studies in the Development of Greek Thought.* Oxford: Oxford University Press, 1999.

Caldwell, Mark H. "Allegory: The Renaissance Mode." *ELH* 44, no. 4 (1977): 580-600.

Cassirer, Ernst. *Language and Myth.* Translated by Susanne K. Langer. New York: Dover, 1946.

——— *Mythical Thought.* Vol. 2 of The Philosophy of Symbolic Forms. Translated by Ralph Manheim. New Haven, CT: Yale University Press, 1955.

Cicero. *Tusculan Disputations.* Translated by J. E. King. Loeb Classical Library. Cambridge, MA: Harvard University Press, 1966.

―――― *On Duties*. Translated by Walter Miller. Loeb Classical Library. Cambridge, MA: Harvard University Press, 1997.

Clifford, Gay. *The Transformations of Allegory*. London: Routledge & Kegan Paul, 1974.

Coleridge, Samuel Taylor. *Miscellaneous Criticism*. Edited by Thomas Middleton Raysor. Cambridge, MA: Harvard University Press, 1936.

Collingwood, R. G., "Plato's Philosophy of Art." *Mind* 34, no. 134 (Apr. 1925): 154-172.

Cornford, Francis M. *From Religion to Philosophy: A Study in the Origins of Western Speculation*. Mineola, NY: Dover Publications, 2004.

―――― *Principium Sapientiae: The Origins of Greek Philosophical Thought*. Cambridge: Cambridge University Press, 1952.

Cowan, Bainard. "Walter Benjamin's Theory of Allegory." *New German Critique*, no. 22 (1981): 109-22.

Crotty, Kevin. *The Philosopher's Song: The Poets' Influence on Plato*. Lanham, MD: Lexington Books, 2009.

Dell Bello, Davide. *Forgotten Paths: Etymology and the Allegorical Mindset*. Washington D.C.: The Catholic University of America Press, 2007.

De Man, Paul. *Blindness and Insight: Essays in the Rhetoric of Contemporary Criticism*. Minneapolis: University of Minnesota Press, 1983.

Destrée, Pierre and Fritz-Gregor Herrmann, editors. *Plato and the Poets*. Leiden: Brill, 2011.

Detienne, Marcel. *The Creation of Mythology*. Translated by Margaret Cook. Chicago: University of Chicago Press, 1986.

―――― *The Masters of Truth in Archaic Greece*. Translated by Janet Lloyd. New York: Zone Books, 1996.

Dodds, E. R. *The Greeks and the Irrational*. Berkeley, CA: University of California Press, 1951.

Edelstein, Ludwig. "The Function of the Myth in Plato's Philosophy." *Journal of the History of Ideas* 10, n. 04 (1949): 463-81.

Eliade, Mircea. *Myth and Reality*. Translated by Willard R. Trask. Long Grove, IL: Waveland Press, 1998.

―――― *The Myth of the Eternal Return: Cosmos and History*. Translated by Willard R. Trask. Princeton, NJ: Princeton University Press, 2005.

Everson, Stephen, editor. *Companions to Ancient Thought 1: Epistemology*. Cambridge: Cambridge University Press, 1990.

Ficino, Marsilio. *Platonic Theology*. Edited by James Hankins and William Bowen. Translated by Michael J. B. Allen and John Warden. Tatti Renaissance Library. Cambridge, MA: Harvard University Press, 2001-2006.

Fletcher, Angus. *Allegory: The Theory of a Symbolic Mode*. Ithaca, NY: Cornell University Press, 1964.

Frankfort, Henri, H. A. Frankfort, John A. Wilson, and Thorkild Jacobsen. *Before Philosophy: The Intellectual Adventure of Early Man*. 1946. Reprint, Baltimore: Penguin, 1949.

Friedländer, Paul. *Plato*. 3 vols. Translated by Hans Meyerhoff. New York: Bollingen, 1958-1969.

Gotshalk, Richard. *Homer and Hesiod, Myth and Philosophy*. Lanham, MD: University Press of America, 2000.

Gould, Thomas. The Ancient Quarrel Between Poetry and Philosophy. Princeton, NJ: Princeton University Press, 1990.

Graham, Daniel W., editor and translator, *The Texts of Early Greek Philosophy: The Complete Fragments and Select Testimonies of the Major Presocratics*. Cambridge: Cambridge University Press, 2010.

Gregory, M. John. "Myth and Transcendence in Plato." *Thought* 43 (1968): 273-96.

Guthrie, W. K. C. *Myth and Reason*. Oration Delivered at the London School of Economics and Political Science on Friday, 12 December, 1952. London: London School of Economics and Political Science, 1953.

Hadot, Pierre. *What is Ancient Philosophy?* Translated by Michael Chase. Cambridge, MA: Harvard University Press, 2002.

Halmi, Nicholas. *The Genealogy of the Romantic Symbol*. Oxford: Oxford University Press, 2008.

Hamlyn, D. W. "*Eikasia* in Plato's *Republic*." *The Philosophical Quarterly* 8 (1958): 14-23.

Harrison, Jane. *Themis*. Whitefish, MT: Kessinger Publishing, 2003.

Hatab, Lawrence J. *Myth and Philosophy: A Contest of Truths*. La Salle, IL: Open Court, 1990.

Hegel, G.W.F. *Phenomenology of Spirit*. Translated by A. V. Miller. Oxford: Oxford University Press, 1977.

Heraclitus. *Homeric Problems*. Edited and translated by Donald A. Russell and David Konstan. Atlanta, GA: Society of Biblical Literature, 2005.

Hesiod. *The Homeric Hymns, Epic Cycle, Homerica*. Translated by Hugh G. Evelyn-White. Cambridge, MA: Harvard University Press, 1914.

Hinks, Roger. *Myth and Allegory in Ancient Art*. London: The Warburg Institute, 1939.

Homer. *Iliad*. Translated by Samuel Butler. Cambridge: Cambridge University Press, 1898.

Honig, Edwin. *Dark Conceit: The Making of Allegory*. Evanston, IL: Northwestern University Press, 1959.

Jaspers, Karl. "The Axial Period." In *The Origin and Goal of History*. Translated by Michael Bullock, 1-21. New Haven, CT: Yale University Press, 1965.

Kirk, G. S., J. E. Raven, and M. Schofield, editors. *The Presocratic Philosophers*. 2nd ed. Cambridge: Cambridge University Press, 1983.

Laks, André. "Between Religion and Philosophy: The Function of Allegory in the 'Derveni Papyrus'." *Phronesis* 42, no. 2 (1997): 121-42.

———, and Glenn W. Most, editors. *Studies on the Derveni Papyrus*. Oxford: Clarendon Press, 1997.

Lamberton, Robert. *Homer the Theologian: Neoplatonist Allegorical Reading and the Growth of the Epic Tradition*. Berkeley, CA: University of California Press, 1986.

Latona, Max. "The Tale is Not My Own: Myth and Recollection in Plato." *Apeiron* 37, no. 3 (2004): 181-210.

Lear, Jonathan. "The Efficacy of Myth in Plato's *Republic*." *Proceedings of the Boston Area Colloquium of Ancient Philosophy* 19, no. 1 (2004): 35-56.

Le Doeuff, Michèle. *The Philosophical Imaginary*. Translated by Colin Gordon. Stanford, CA: Stanford University Press, 1989.

Lesher, J. H. "Perceiving and Knowing in the 'Iliad' and 'Odyssey'." *Phronesis: A Journal of Ancient Philosophy* 26 (1981): 2-24.

Levin, Susan B. *The Ancient Quarrel Between Philosophy and Poetry Revisited: Plato and the Greek Literary Tradition*. Oxford: Oxford University Press, 2001.

Lévi-Strauss, Claude. *Myth and Meaning: Cracking the Code of Culture*. New York: Schocken Books, 1979.

Lewis, C. S. The Allegory of Love: A Study in Medieval Tradition. Oxford: Oxford University Press, 1967.

Lewis, Rhodri. "Francis Bacon, Allegory and the Uses of Myth." *The Review of English Studies* 61, no. 250 (2010): 360-389.

Long, A. A. "The scope of early Greek philosophy." In *The Cambridge Companion to Early Greek Philosophy*, edited by A. A. Long, 1-21. Cambridge: Cambridge University Press, 1999.

———. "Stoic Readings of Homer." In *Stoic Studies*, edited by A. A. Long, 58-84. Cambridge: Cambridge University Press, 1996.

Machosky, Brenda. *Structures of Appearing: Allegory and the Work of Literature*. New York: Fordham University Press, 2013.

McCabe, Mary Margaret. "Myth, Allegory and Argument in Plato." *Apeiron* 25, no. 4 (December 1992) 47-68.

McKeon, Richard, editor. *The Basic Works of Aristotle*. New York: Modern Library, 2001.

Morgan, Kathryn A. *Myth and Philosophy from the Presocratics to Plato*. Cambridge: Cambridge University Press, 2000.

Most, Glenn. "The Poetics of Early Greek Philosophy." In *The Cambridge Companion to Early Greek Philosophy*, edited by A. A. Long, 332-62. Cambridge: Cambridge University Press, 1999.

Murray, Penelope. "What is a Muthos for Plato?" In *From Myth to Reason? Studies in the Development of Greek Thought*, edited by Richard Buxton, 251-62. Oxford: Oxford University Press, 1999.

Naddaf, Gerard. "Allegory and the Origins of Philosophy." In *Logos & Muthos: Philosophical Essays in Greek Literature*, edited by William Wians, 99-132. Albany, NY: SUNY Press, 2010.

Nightingale, Andrea Wilson. "The Philosophers in Archaic Greek Culture." In *The Cambridge Companion to Archaic Greece*, edited by H. A. Shapiro, 169-98. Cambridge: Cambridge University Press, 2007.

Obbink, Dirk. "Allegory and Exegesis in the Derveni Papyrus: The Origin of Greek Exegesis." In *Metaphor, Allegory & The Classical Tradition*, edited by G. R. Boys-Stones, 177-88. Oxford: Oxford University Press, 2003.

Palmer, John. *Parmenides and Presocratic Philosophy*. Oxford: Oxford University Press, 2009.

Payen, J.C. "Genèse et finalités de la pensée allégorique au Moyen Age." *Revue de métaphysique et de morale* 78 (1973): 466-79.

Pépin, Jean. *Mythe et allégorie: Les origines grecques et les contestations judéo-chrétiennes*. Paris: Aubier, Éditions Montaigne, 1958.

Pico della Mirandola, Giovanni. "Oration on the Dignity of Man." In *The Renaissance Philosophy of Man*. Edited by Ernst Cassirer, Paul Oskar Kristeller, and John Herman Randall, Jr. Translated by Elizabeth Livermore Forbes. Chicago: University of Chicago Press, 1956.

Plato. *Plato: Complete Works*. Edited by John M. Cooper. Indianapolis: Hackett, 1997.

Popper, Karl. "Back to the Pre-Socratics: The Presidential Address." *Proceedings of the Aristotelian Society* 59 (1958-59): 1-24.

Porphyry. *On the Cave of the Nymphs*. Translated by Robert Lamberton. Barryton, NY: Midpoint Trade Books, 1983.

Proclus. *Theology of Plato*. Translated by Thomas Taylor. London: Prometheus Trust, 1816.

Prudentius. *Volume 1*. Translated by H. J. Thomson. Loeb Classical Library 387. Cambridge, MA: Harvard University Press, 1949.

Quilligan, Maureen. *The Language of Allegory: Defining the Genre*. Ithaca, NY: Cornell University Press, 1979.

Radin, Paul. *Primitive Man as Philosopher*. New York: D. Appleton & Co., 1927.

Rosen, Stanley. *The Quarrel Between Philosophy and Poetry*. New York: Routledge, 1988.

Schelling, F.W.J. *Historical-critical Introduction to the Philosophy of Mythology*. Translated by Mason Richey and Markus Zisselsberger. Albany: SUNY Press, 2007.

Silvestris, Bernard. *Cosmographia*. Translated by Winthrop Wetherbee. New York: Columbia University Press, 1973.

Smith, Janet E. "Plato's Use of Myth in the Education of Philosophic Man." *Phoenix* 40, no. 1 (Spring 1986): 20-34.

Snell, Bruno. *The Discovery of Mind: The Greek Origins of European Thought.* Translated by T.G. Rosenmeyer. Cambridge: Harvard University Press, 1953.

Sproul, Barbara C. *Primal Myths: Creating the World.* San Francisco: Harper & Row, 1979.

Stambovsky, Phillip. *Myth and the Limits of Reason.* Lanham, MD: University Press of America, 2004.

Stewart, John Alexander. *The Myths of Plato.* New York: Macmillan & Co., 1905.

Stewart, Robert Scott. "The Epistemological Function of Platonic Myth. *Philosophy & Rhetoric* 22, no. 4 (1989): 260-80.

Struck, Peter. *Birth of the Symbol: Ancient Readers at the Limits of Their Texts.* New Jersey: Princeton University Press, 2004.

Tambling, Jeremy. *Allegory.* New York: Routledge, 2010.

Tate, J. "The Beginnings of Greek Allegory." *The Classical Review* 41, no. 6 (Dec. 1927): 214-15.

——— "Plato and Allegorical Interpretation." *The Classical Quarterly* 23, no. 3/4 (Jul. – Oct. 1929): 142-54.

——— "Plato and Allegorical Interpretation." *The Classical Quarterly* 24, no. 1 (Jan. 1930): 1-10.

——— "On the History of Allegorism." *The Classical Quarterly* 28 no. 2 (Apr. 1934) 105-14.

Tejera, Victor. "Irony and Allegory in the 'Phaedrus'." *Philosophy & Rhetoric* 8 (Spring 1975): 71-87.

Todorov, Tzvetan. *Theories of the Symbol.* Translated by Catherine Porter. Ithaca, NY: Cornell University Press, 1982.

Verdenius, W. J. "Notes on the Proem of Hesiod's *Theogony*." *Mnemosyne* 4, no. 25 (1972): 225-60.

Verene, Donald Phillip. *Vico's Science of Imagination.* Ithaca, NY: Cornell University Press, 1981.

——— *Philosophy and the Return to Self-Knowledge.* New Haven, CT: Yale University Press, 1997.

——— *Knowledge of Things Human and Divine: Vico's* New Science *and* Finnegans Wake. New Haven, CT: Yale University Press, 2003.

——— *Speculative Philosophy.* Lanham, MD: Lexington Books, 2009.

Vernant, Jean-Pierre. *Myth and Thought Among the Greeks.* Translated by Janet Lloyd. New York: Zone Books, 2006.

Vico, Giambattista. *The New Science.* Translated by Thomas Goddard Bergin and Max Harold Fisch. Ithaca: Cornell University Press, 1984.

Vives, Juan Luis. "Fable About Man." In *The Renaissance Philosophy of Man*. Edited by Ernst Cassirer, Paul Oskar Kristeller, and John Herman Randall Jr. Translated by Nancy Lenkeith. Chicago: Chicago University Press, 1956.

Westcott, Brooke Foss. *Essays in the History of Religious Thought in the West*. London: Macmillan & Co., 1891.

Wheelright, Philip. *Metaphor and Reality*. Bloomington, IN: Indiana University Press, 1962.

——— *The Burning Fountain: A Study in the Language of Symbolism*. Bloomington, IN: Indiana University Press, 1968.

Whitehead, Alfred North. *Aims of Education and Other Essays*. New York: The Free Press, 1967.

Whitman, Jon. *Allegory: The Dynamics of an Ancient and Medieval Technique*. Cambridge, MA: Harvard University Press, 1987.

———, editor. *Interpretation and Allegory: Antiquity to the Modern Period*. Leiden: Brill, 2000.

Wians, William, ed. *Logos & Muthos: Philosophical Essays in Greek Literature*. Albany, NY: SUNY Press, 2010.

Index

A
Adeimantus 90
Aesop 22
Alcibiades 81
Anaxagoras 45, 61, 67, 71
   Nous 48, 64
   allegoresis 73–74
Anaximander 31–32, 44, 60, 75
   apeiron 48, 64
   use of allegory 66–70
Anaximenes 44, 54, 70
   aer 48, 64, 68-69
Aquinas, Thomas 87
Aristotle 44, 60, 101
   history of allegory 14–15
   muthos/logos 37, 47–49
   on philosophy 42, 46
   mimesis 87–88, 90
Augustine, Saint 87

B
Benjamin, Walter 21
Boreas 107
Bundy, Murray W. 95–97, 100

C
Cassirer, Ernst 27-28
Cicero 16, 86–87
Clement (of Alexandria) 42
Coleridge, Samuel Taylor 20
Collingwood, R. G. 93
Cornford, F. M. 30–32, 36–37
Cowan, Bainard 21

D
Diogenes (of Apollonia) 61, 67, 71, 74–75
Diotima 81, 94

E
Edelstein, Ludwig 85–86, 107
Empedocles 13, 45, 47
   epic simile 36, 54–55
   poetics 63–65, 67
   use of allegory 75–77

F
Frankfort, Henri 25–29, 45–47, 69–70
Friedländer, Paul 83–84, 99

G
Glaucon 95
Goethe, Johann Wolfgang von 20
Gorgias 62

H
Hadot, Pierre 81–82, 84
Halmi, Nicholas 20
Hecataeus (of Miletus) 56
Hegel, G. W. F. 23, 84
Heraclitus 42–45, 48, 52, 54, 56
   critique of the poets 49–50, 86, 89
   poetics 59–60, 63–67
   use of allegory 70–71, 75
Hesiod 26, 29, 32, 33
   allegoresis 13, 66–77
   Presocratics 41–49, 55–58
   poetics 59, 61–65
   Plato 79–80, 86, 89, 101–4
Hinks, Roger 35
Hippias (of Elis) 62
Homer 29, 33, 36, 101
   allegoresis 12–13, 15, 67–76
   Presocratics 41–49
   epistemology 50–58
   poetics 59, 61–65
   Plato 79–80, 86, 89, 101–4
Hussey, Edward 51

I
Ion (the rhapsode) 103

J
Jaeger, Werner 41
Jaspers, Karl 35–36
Jove 98

K
Kirk, G. S. 49, 52, 55, 76

L
Langland, William 22
Latona, Max 99
Lesher, J. H. 52
Leucippus 45
Lewis, C. S. 11
Long, A. A. 55–56, 72

M
Man, Paul de 20
Melissus (of Samos) 45
Metrodorus (of Lampsacus) 67, 71, 74
Mnemosyne 51, 99
Morgan, Kathryn A. 12–13, 62, 73, 77
Most, Glenn W. 58–59, 61–66, 71, 76
Murray, Penelope 105

N
Naddaf, Gerard 72, 75
Nightingale, Andrea 43, 48

O
Odysseus 52
Orithuia 107
Orpheus 74

P
Parmenides 13, 44–45
  poetics 63, 65, 67
  use of allegory 75–77
Penia 82

Phaedrus 94, 106–7
Pherecydes (of Soros) 13, 45, 61, 67, 71–72, 75
Plato 24, 41–49, 67, 77
  history of allegory 13–15, 39
  poetics 59–60
  philosophical myth 79–86
  quarrel with the poets 86–92
  mimesis 93–100
  use of allegory 100–11
Plutarch 13
Popper, Karl 57, 60
Poros 82
Porphyry 72
Prodicus 62
Protagoras 47, 62
Pythagoras 42, 44–45, 56

Q
Quintilian 16

S
Schelling, F. W. J. 20, 38–39
Simonides 47
Simplicius 69
Snell, Bruno 36, 53–55, 57, 85
Socrates 41–42, 94–96
  as philosopher 81–84
  quarrel with the poets 89–91
  divine inspiration 103
  on allegory 106–7
Spenser, Edmund 22
Stewart, J. A. 104–6, 109–11,

T
Tate, Jonathan 12, 71–73, 108
Thales 30–31, 44, 60, 70
  water 48, 68
Theagenes (of Rhegium) 13, 45
  poetics 59, 61
  allegoresis 67, 71–72
Theophrastus 48
Todorov, Tzvetan 20

V

Verene, Donald Phillip 37, 93, 98
   speculative philosophy 23, 28, 82, 88
Vico, Giambattista 98–100
Vives, Juan Luis 87

W

Westcott, Brooke 110–11
Whitehead, Alfred North 40
Whitman, Jon 83
Wordsworth, William 79

X

Xenophanes 43–44, 52, 56
   critique of the poets 50, 86, 89
   poetics 59–60, 63–67
   use of allegory 70–71, 75–76

Z

Zeno (of Elea) 45, 65
Zeus 74

ibidem.eu